ADAM HAMILTON

WHEN CHRISTIANS GET IT WRONG

Abingdon Press

Nashville

WHEN CHRISTIANS GET IT WRONG

This book is printed on acid-free paper.

Library of Congress Cataloging-in-Publication Data

Hamilton, Adam, 1964–
    When Christians get it wrong / Adam Hamilton.
        p.   cm.
    ISBN 978-1-4267-0914-2 (book- pbk./trade pbk. : alk. paper) 1.
Apologetics.   2. Christian life.   I. Title.
    BT1103.H35   2010
    239′.7—dc22

                                                                2010019358

Scripture quotations unless noted otherwise are taken from the New Revised Standard Version of the Bible, copyright 1989 by the Division of Christian Education of the National Council of the Churches of Christ in the United States of America. Used by permission. All rights reserved.

Scripture quotations marked NIV are taken from the Holy Bible, NEW INTERNATIONAL VERSION®. Copyright © 1973, 1978, 1984 by the International Bible Society. All rights reserved throughout the world. Used by permission of the International Bible Society.

10 11 12 13 14 15 16 17 18 19—10 9 8 7 6 5 4 3 2 1

MANUFACTURED IN THE UNITED STATES OF AMERICA

To John

CONTENTS

INTRODUCTION

This book was born out of a conversation with a young man who had some pretty strong negative perceptions of the Christian faith. As I listened to him, I realized that he was rejecting a God that I, too, had rejected years earlier. He described many of the same frustrations I had as a pastor with how Christians sometimes act and with the beliefs about God that many Christians hold.

Later that same year (2007), David Kinnaman and Gabe Lyon published the results of their research with young adults who are disengaged from the church—men and women like John—and their findings closely mirrored John's concerns. Kinnaman and Lyon's book, *unChristian*, focused largely on the attitudes and behaviors exhibited by some Christians that young adults found off-putting. They found that 91 percent of young adults who are not involved in church described Christians as anti-homosexual, 87 percent of them described Christians as judgmental, and 85 percent of them described Christians as hypocritical.[1]

Kinnaman and Lyon and a host of others have focused on the attitudes and actions of Christians that have turned young adults away from the Christian faith. But my conversation with John, and with a number of other young adults, indicates that it is not only the attitudes and actions of Christians that are off-putting but also the theological convictions that often give rise to these actions. John and other young adults I have spoken with take issue with Christian *doctrine* (or belief) as it has been expressed to them by many Christians—doctrines related to suffering, science and faith, the Bible, salvation, and the final judgment, particularly as it relates to non-Christians.

In this book I seek to address both the attitudes and actions of Christians who get it wrong *and* the beliefs that are most often cited as problematic by non-Christians. At the end of each chapter, I also offer suggestions on what it looks like when Christians get it right.

This book is for two audiences: The first is young adults who are turning away from Christianity in larger numbers than previous generations did at the same age and stage in life. I hope the book will be read by college students and young adults who don't go to church, who have been frustrated and turned off by what they have heard from and experienced with Christians. The second audience is Christians; I invite them to examine their attitudes, actions, and beliefs. I offer a different way of understanding some very serious theological issues— related to the nature of God, Scripture, science and faith, the religions of the world, and homosexuality—from what is often articulated by the loudest Christian voices in the current culture.

A companion video and leader's guide are available for use with book clubs, campus ministries, small groups, and Sunday school classes. I also hope that churches might make this a six-week study, with pastors preaching on each topic as I did in 2009.

I am grateful for the team at Abingdon Press. They have been patient, encouraging, and tremendously helpful in bringing this book to publication. I am honored to be in partnership and ministry with them. Thank you!

I hope and pray that this book will help some young adults find faith once more and become followers of Jesus Christ. It is also my hope that the book might chart a path for Christians in how we can "get it right." Churches that "get it wrong" may lose an entire generation of young adults, the future of the church. Those that get it right have a "future with hope" (Jeremiah 29:11).

Adam Hamilton
March 2010

NOTE

1. See David Kinnaman and Gabe Lyon, *unChristian* (Grand Rapids, Mich.: Baker Books, 2007), or visit www.unchristian.com.

CHAPTER 1

WHEN CHRISTIANS ARE UNCHRISTIAN

John was twenty-four years old and had just returned from six years as an Army Airborne Ranger deployed first in Afghanistan and then in Iraq. It was John's dad, Tom, who suggested we meet. I am Tom's pastor. Tom told me that John had very strong negative feelings about the Christian faith. He felt that both John and I would benefit from a conversation together. We met in my office, and in our ninety-minute conversation John was thoughtful, articulate, and respectful, but at times almost angry as he described for me the reasons he had rejected Christianity. His subtle undertone of anger was not directed toward me, but at the views, attitudes, and actions of Christians he had known—views that seemed out of sync with the God of love that Christianity preached. John was describing for me the ways in which he believed Christians get it wrong.

John's feelings about Christians were not new to me. I had heard them many times before, though seldom as thoughtfully or comprehensively presented as John presented them. I had felt some of these same things myself in dealing with some of my fellow Christians. Several years after meeting John, our church set up a Web site to invite young adults (those under thirty-five) to tell us where they believe Christians get it wrong. About that same time we began sitting down to talk with people who had opted out of church. There were so many common responses between the two groups. Generally we found that young people rejected Christianity because of the beliefs, attitudes, and actions of Christians they knew.

Their criticism of Christianity usually included one or more of five key themes: (1) the unchristian ways some Christians act, (2) the anti-intellectual, anti-science stance of some Christians, (3) Christianity's views of other world religions, (4) questions related to the role of God in human suffering, and (5) the way Christians view homosexuality. Each of these themes will be considered in a chapter in this book.

My hope in writing this book is to speak for young adults who have been turned off, frustrated, or even hurt by Christians and to suggest what Christianity might look like when Christians get it right. Let's begin with the unchristian ways some Christians act.

WHEN CHRISTIANS ARE UNCHRISTIAN

In their 2007 book, *unChristian* (Baker Books), David Kinnaman and Gabe Lyons outlined the research of the Barna Group with hundreds of young adults who, like John in our opening story, were outside the Christian faith. They found that more young adults today are turning away from Christianity than in years past. Their research did not explore the theological issues that have turned people away from the Christian faith; instead they focused on understanding the perceptions non-Christian young adults have of Christians. Among their findings:

- 91% of those adults surveyed who were outside the Christian faith felt Christians were "anti-homosexual."
- 87% felt Christians were judgmental.
- 85% felt Christians were hypocritical.
- 75% felt Christians were too political.
- 70% thought Christians were insensitive.

My conversations with young adults substantiate these findings. If these words accurately describe how young adults have experienced Christians, then is it any surprise that they are turning away from the Christian faith in droves?

When I ask non-Christians what they think Jesus stood for, most say, "Love." And they are correct; this is one of the defining elements of Jesus' teaching. He told his followers that God's will for humanity could be summarized with two commands: love God and love your neighbor. He went on to say that our neighbor is anyone who needs our help. The love we are to

> SOME OF the most insensitive, critical, judgmental, and mean-spirited people I've known claimed to be committed Christians.

show is not a feeling but a way of acting—a love of kindness and compassion and a desire to bless and seek good for others. Jesus told his disciples they were to love not only their neighbors and friends but their enemies as well. He told them that the world would know that they are his disciples by their love. Non-Christians know that Jesus stood for love. Which is why, when those who claim to follow Jesus act in unloving ways, it feels particularly unpleasant.

This disparity between the love Christians are meant to display and what young adults often experience is most pronounced when Christians speak with judgment or in disparaging ways toward others.

One young man described an experience when he was invited to attend a special youth group event at a big church in his town. He noted that the kids at school rarely spoke to him until it was "bring a friend day" at youth group. They invited him to join their group at the local water park. Here's his description of how the day went:

> It didn't start off badly; the rides at the park were fun, and I even enjoyed hanging out with some of them. But during the long ride back to the church, they started talking about people. They discussed who was having sex, who was smoking weed, who was gay. The more they talked the worse things they said. Many of the people they were talking about were my friends, and they knew it! To make things worse, some of the ones

talking loudest were doing the very things they were gossiping about. Finally, they got on to the subject of who was going to hell. It seems that if you didn't go to their brand of church, you didn't stand a chance of getting into heaven. That, of course, meant me, and it didn't seem to matter to them at all that I was sitting right there, soaking all this up.

The judgmental, hypocritical, and unloving spirit these Christians displayed left this young man determined not to go back to church.

Another young woman echoed these same sentiments when she said:

> I'm thinking of the Christians in my school that I see every day. They judge everyone constantly. It's annoying, and a lot of people don't really like it or like them because of it. I have a really good friend who claims to be a really hard-core Christian but he smokes weed all the time and drinks and does all these things and lies, and he's just not a Christian at all.

These were both teens who turned away from the Christian faith because of the actions of Christians they knew. But this phenomenon is not unique to young adults. No doubt you can think of examples of Christians you have known who were judgmental, hypocritical, and unloving.

Some of the most insensitive, critical, judgmental, and mean-spirited people I've known were persons who claimed to be committed Christians.

I was officiating at the graveside

FOLLOWING THE funeral, some relatives of one of the boy's parents came to me and asked, "Why didn't you tell them that their son is in hell today?"

funeral for a young man who had taken his own life. The parents were still in shock and experiencing intense grief. In the eulogy and message I sought to help them and all who had gathered to make sense of this terrible tragedy while finding comfort and hope in God. As a part of the service we remembered the unique and special qualities of their son. Following the service, a husband and wife— sister and brother-in-law of one of the boy's parents— came to me and asked, "Why didn't you tell them that their son is in hell today?" I was taken aback and asked, "How do you know the boy is in hell today? Do you know what was in the boy's heart? Are you so certain you know the mind of God?" They looked at me and walked away. What kind of people are so certain of another's eternal fate that they can stand before grieving parents and callously tell them their son is in hell?

I could fill this book with stories like these from my own personal experience of Christians, including a few pastors I know, who are free with their condemnation of everyone who doesn't conform to their very narrow view of the world, of the Bible, and of truth.

JESUS AND THE PHARISEES

Of course Jesus confronted the same kinds of things in his day. If you read the Gospels carefully, Jesus never got angry with prostitutes, adulterers, or ordinary "sinners." Nor did his actions turn such people away. In fact, Jesus drew "sinners" to himself by the thousands. He made such people feel at ease. The only people Jesus had words of judgment for in the Gospels were the *religious* folks. What angered him the most about these people, particularly the religious leaders, was their judgmentalism, their hypocrisy, and their failure to love. They believed God was primarily interested in people following the rules. Jesus taught that God's primary rule was love, and that God's interest wasn't in condemning "sinners" but in drawing them to God.

Though Jesus was opposed by various people in the Gospels, his primary opposition was from a group of religious people called *Pharisees* (the word likely comes from a Hebrew word that means "set apart" or "separated"). They believed that holiness and a life pleasing to God came from separating yourself from sin and in obeying the commands of God. This all makes sense but, like many modern-day Christians, they had missed the point. They failed to see that God's primary concern is not rules, but people. They should have been celebrating the fact that thousands of people who had turned away from organized religion were drawn to hear Jesus teach about the kingdom of God. Instead they were repulsed by Jesus' willingness to associate with people "like that." In response, Jesus spoke some pretty harsh words to the Pharisees and the other religious leaders of his time. The word he used most frequently to describe them in the Gospels is the Greek word *hupokrisis* from which we have the word *hypocrisy*. The Greek word was used to refer to an actor in a play— a pretender.

The truth is, we are all in danger of being "pretenders" when it comes to our highest values and aspirations. This is particularly true for religious people, which is why Jesus often warned his disciples about hypocrisy, warnings that covered four different expressions of hypocrisy: wrong motives, judging others, "majoring in the minors," and being two-faced. Let's briefly consider what Jesus warned against in each of these areas.

> **IN ESSENCE**
>
> Jesus was saying, "Stop pointing out the sins of others; you've got enough issues of your own!"

1. WRONG MOTIVES

Once when Jesus was talking to his followers, he warned them about the dangers of praying, fasting, and helping out the poor. Why would he do that? Aren't all of those good things? Yes they are, unless you do them for the wrong reasons. If you pray and fast out of a genuine desire to get closer to God, you do well. The same is true if you give money to the poor because you sincerely wish to lessen their burdens.

But that's not why everyone does these things. Jesus talked about people who would pray on street corners, blow a loud trumpet when they were about to give to a needy person, and make sure everyone who saw them knew they were fasting. Why? So that other people (people like them) would know how "religious" they were, and praise them for it. They were using God and their religion to further their careers, or their stature in the community, or to meet their needs for affirmation from others (see Matthew 6:1-8, 16-18).

2. POINTING OUT THE SIN OF OTHERS WITHOUT SEEING OUR OWN

One of the strangest things Jesus ever said had to do with lumber (makes sense coming from a carpenter, doesn't it?). He asked some religious leaders how they could criticize people who had a speck of sawdust in their eye, while the leaders didn't notice the two-by-four lodged in their own eyes (Matthew 7:1-5). What did he mean? He was referring to religious people who readily point out the sins of others while failing to see their own shortcomings. They demonstrate a kind of superiority and spiritual or moral pride, but they fail to see that their pride is actually a more sinister and deadly sin than the sins of those they are denouncing. Jesus then called his hearers to remove the "log" from their own eye before seeking to remove the speck from another's eye. In essence he was saying, "Stop pointing out the sins of others; you've got enough issues of your own!"

3. MAJORING IN MINORS

If you grew up where and when Jesus did, you were encouraged to *tithe*, that is, contribute a tenth of your income to support the Temple and other religious causes. Some of Jesus' religious contemporaries had this figured out in great detail. You know those herbs you grow on your windowsill, the little ones? Well these folks would even take the clippings from those plants, separate out a tenth of them, and contribute even that. No one was going to accuse them of not living up to their obligations!

Jesus did, however. Calling them "blind guides," he reminded them that while tithing is good, they were missing the more important matters like living a life of justice and mercy toward their neighbors (Matthew 23:23-24).

I've known people who called themselves Christians, who were convinced that they alone were right, and who were willing to fight over the tiniest, least consequential of things. We Christians argue over forms of baptism, our interpretation of minor points of Scripture, even the forms of music we play in church. Christians have fought entire wars over our sectarian differences, all the while forgetting that Jesus said that the defining characteristic of a Christian's life is meant to be love.

> **TOO MANY**
> Christians fail to let their faith change their values, their hearts, and ultimately their daily lives.

4. BEING TWO-FACED

....

You probably know people who appear to be one thing when you first meet them, but upon getting to know them better you find they are something else entirely. Jesus knew people like this, too. He once suggested that such people are like a person who washes the outside of a dirty cup but fails to wash the inside, so the drink that remains inside the cup spoils—I picture the glasses of milk or soda I used to find in my teenage daughter's room that had been sitting there for weeks—curdled, moldy, and with the rankest of smells (Luke 11:39)!

Jesus was speaking of a superficial faith, which is seen in the outward appearance of religious behavior but has not sunk down into the heart. Like those who focus on the minutiae, these people have missed the bigger point of faith. Their religion is skin deep and hasn't addressed the really serious issues in their hearts or the truly important issues of society. Not all

IT IS

so easy to do the right things for all the wrong reasons. It is so easy to point out the sins of others while ignoring our own. Most of us are experts at "majoring in the minors."

Pharisees were hypocrites, but many seemed to miss the point in this way.

This description also applies to too many Christians I know. They understand how to do religious things but fail to let their religion change their values, their hearts, and ultimately their daily lives. Their religion is window dressing.

In a prophetic warning to his disciples, Jesus says in Luke 12:1, "Beware of the yeast of the Pharisees, that is, their hypocrisy." Why did Jesus warn the disciples against becoming hypocrites? Because he knew that his own followers would not be immune to this common temptation for religious people.

WE ARE ALL RECOVERING PHARISEES

Today's Pharisees are religious people who struggle with wrong motives, with being critical and judgmental of others, with missing the point, and with being two-faced. Unfortunately, I've got to confess, I am a recovering Pharisee—one who

> **WHEN CHRISTIANS**
> are judgmental,
> hypocritical, insensitive,
> and mean-spirited, they
> are acting in ways that
> are *un*christian.

often falls off the wagon. Everyone I know, religious people and atheists alike, struggle with these four tendencies.

It is so easy to do the right things for all the wrong reasons. It is so easy to point out the sins of others while ignoring our own. Most of us are experts at "majoring in the minors" while failing to do the really important things God demands of us. And which of us has never put on a face and pretended to be something we're not? It is only in recognizing our tendency to be Pharisees that we have any hope of remaining in recovery.

My experience with non-religious people is that they do not expect Christians to be perfect. In fact, one young adult said, "I don't mind that you Christians don't live up to your ideals. I don't live up to all of my ideals either. In the end, I guess we're all hypocrites. It's just that I and my friends recognize that we're hypocrites. It seems that many Christians haven't figured this out yet." Again, the hypocrisy of Christians is most troubling to new Christians when we point out the sins of others.

GETTING IT RIGHT

Every Christian gets it wrong sometimes. The critique from John in our opening story and from the countless others who share with him a frustration with Christian

> **THERE REALLY** are countless Christians who daily seek to live authentic lives of faith.

hypocrisy is an important wake-up call—a warning to Christians who are becoming the very Pharisees Jesus preached against.

When Christians are judgmental, hypocritical, insensitive, and mean-spirited, they are acting in ways that are *un*christian. When the apostle Paul described what Christians should strive to be like, he used these words: love, joy, peace, patience, kindness, gentleness, generosity, faithfulness, and self-control (Galatians 5:22-23). Unchristian Christians stand out because even non-Christians know that these people are living in a way that is inconsistent with Jesus' teaching. Jesus commanded his followers not to judge. He warned them against hypocrisy. Again and again he called them to love all, both their neighbors and those with whom they did not see eye to eye.

For all the Christians who get it wrong, I believe there are many who get it right. They are not as vocal as their pharisaic counterparts. And they are not perfect. But there really are countless Christians who daily seek to live authentic lives of faith. They go out of their way to care for others. They are compassionate. They live and give sacrificially to others. They volunteer their time to serve the poor, or visit the sick, or take the time to encourage the discouraged. They work for justice. They genuinely love people.

When I asked John if he knew any Christians like this he spoke about Margie, a friend he described as "the real thing." She cared about John. She did not judge him. She is a thoughtful, intelligent, and committed Christian who has shown love to John whether he became a Christian or not.

When I think of Christians who get it right, I think of Kathy. She cuts hair in a salon in the basement of her home and I sit in her barber chair once a month. I go as much to be inspired as I do to have my hair cut. This woman has a heart of compassion that won't quit. Every month she shares a story of some project she hopes our church will get behind. Since she has scissors in her hands, I'm all ears! She has started and organized a variety of ministries to care for the homeless in our city. Perhaps my favorite is her work in cutting the hair of the homeless. I had never thought about where the homeless go for a haircut. But Kathy did. She had our church install chairs and sinks at several of the city's missions. Then she organized a team of barbers and stylists to go to these different missions throughout the month to offer free haircuts. She said:

Adam, most of these men haven't had another human being touch them in years. But when they sit in my chair, they are inviting me to touch them. I can feel them tense up at first, and then they relax. My prayer is that somehow, as I am touching them, cutting and styling their hair, they feel God's love for them through me. I don't care what they've done in the past, or whether they've bathed, or how they ended up homeless. I know their lives matter to God and that they are valuable to him. . . . When I am finished, I can see a visible change in these men and women. They look at themselves in the mirror as they rise from my chair and I sense that they remember that they are somebody— that their lives have value—all because of a haircut.

I think that's what it looks like when Christians get it right.

When Christians get it right they love and give, they work for justice and demonstrate kindness. When Christians get it right they, like Jesus, befriend those who are outside the church rather than condemning them. And when Christians get it right, people are drawn to, rather than repelled by, their faith.

NOTE

1. *unChristian*, 28.

CHAPTER 2
·······································
CHRISTIANS, SCIENCE, AND POLITICS

SCIENCE, FAITH, AND FEAR
···

As John and I talked, he told me that it was not just the hypocrisy of Christians that troubled him. He was also turned off by the way many Christians approached modern science. John noted:

The whole question of creationism versus evolution and scientific theory is always something that bothered me. You know that people will tell you God created all of this ten thousand years ago in the blink of an eye; there you go. But when you honestly look at science and evolution—the miraculous complexity of it all and the beauty of how the system works— I've actually asked people, "Don't you see anything divine in that?" "Oh no, no, no." And people will pass off the creation story in the blink of an eye because it's accepted and it's in the Bible. Well you know what, there are a lot of things in the Bible that were written two thousand years ago; and how can we honestly interpret what those men were saying in modern terminology? When people tell me creationism is in the Bible, that is just a statement to me of how exceedingly ignorant someone is. I don't like to blatantly label people as idiots, but I think of them as less intellectually active.

This is the perception many thinking people have of Christians—that they are "less intellectually active."

To hear some Christians talk, you would think we are starring in our own version of the movie *Groundhog Day,* waking up morning after morning to find that it's June 22,

> **SIMPLY PUT,**
>
> Christians are afraid that science will disprove or debunk what they believe.

1633. That's when a tribunal of the church pronounced Galileo a heretic for promoting the shocking notion that the earth moves around the sun, not the other way around. They made Galileo take back what he had said (which he seems to have done with his fingers crossed behind his back), and then placed him under house arrest to prevent him from spreading any more dangerous ideas.

Today, of course, it is common and accepted knowledge that the sun sits at the center of our solar system, and that there are likely countless other solar systems with planets also circling their own stars among all the galaxies flung throughout the universe. In other words, what was a dangerous and heretical idea on June 22, 1633, is now something most people (including most Christians) take for granted. I wonder how many of the issues over which Christians battle with science today will take a similar path.

If Christian attitudes toward science bother you, then you are not alone. Surveys of young adults show that many bright, thinking people find themselves increasingly alienated by the belief, expressed by some Christians, that much of what we know from modern science is incompatible with Christian teaching. This is not a new development, of course. Galileo's trial was only the start of an accelerating process in which scientific discoveries have drawn the wrath of Christians who complain that the new ideas undermine their faith. From discoveries in geology about the age of the earth to the much-maligned science of evolution, some Christians have been pushing back at advances in science for centuries.

As I try to understand why so many Christians carry on this battle with science, I keep coming back to one word: *fear*. Simply put, Christians are afraid that science will disprove or debunk what they believe. They secretly worry that the next scientific development will be the one that decisively shows that God doesn't exist, that the gospel is a fraud. They think that the more people know about science, the less they will believe in God. Christians fear science because they think that it either competes with faith or is actively engaged in destroying faith. They think that science leaves no room for God; if you let it get its foot in the door, science will take over the whole house.

But God is not threatened by science. If creation is the handiwork of God, and science helps us see the exquisite and marvelous workings of creation, how can that do anything but magnify God for people of faith?

Several years ago I had the opportunity to visit the Sistine Chapel in Rome. As I stood there looking up at Michelangelo's magnificent frescoes on the chapel ceiling, a docent came up and asked if I'd like to know more about the work. I said, "Please. I know a little, but I'd like to know more!" She told me that Michelangelo labored for four years to complete the work, and that it is considered one of the most important works in the history of art. She described techniques Michelangelo used, some of which he pioneered, in order to leave such a legacy. She even told me that one of the "facts" I had always been taught about the painting was wrong—Michelangelo did not lie on his back to paint; he stood on the scaffolding and cocked his head back (a far more uncomfortable position)! Do you think I was less in awe by virtue of having the docent's explanations? The docent's insights and knowledge led me to an immensely greater appreciation of the Sistine Ceiling and Michelangelo's artistry.

In the same way, scientists act as God's docents, whether they believe in God or not. By helping us understand God's handiwork, they add to the majesty and glory of creation that, as a believer, leaves me with a greater sense of awe about the One who created all things.

I am an amateur astronomer. I have an 8" Meade LX90 Schmidt-Cassegraine telescope at home that I take out to my backyard to tour the galaxy on warm nights. I begin with a glance at Saturn's rings and Jupiter's moons, but then I head off to the Hercules Cluster and then view a variety of nebula, stars, and galaxies. I turn my scope toward the Milky Way's nearest neighbor, the Andromeda Galaxy. Through my scope it is only a small gray smudge. But here's what I find mindboggling: The light in that smudge took two million years to reach my eye, traveling at the rate of 186,000 miles per second! And this is our nearest neighbor—part of the "local group" of galaxies. And here's how I feel as I stand in the darkness of my backyard: I feel small, and that leads me to realize how truly big God is. Astronomy leads me to say with the psalmist, "The heavens are telling the glory of God" (Psalm 19:1). I stand in the backyard and find myself driven to awe and wonder and praise.

When some Christians add up the ages represented by the genealogies of the Old Testament and then tell us that the earth is less than ten thousand years old, I want to laugh or cry. With John, I find myself wondering why they can't appreciate that the biblical stories of creation were written in the form of Hebrew poetry. They were not written as God's way of giving ancient people a lesson in cosmology or biology or physics. They were written to say that behind all of the magnificent beauty of creation there is One who created—who called for all that is and gave it form and shape and established the laws and patterns that govern it.

In the twentieth century, many Christians opposed

evolution. Not all Christians held this opinion, but some of the most vocal Christians did. They felt that evolution (at least at the "macro" level) somehow

USING THE Bible to answer scientific questions is a bit like trying to use a paintbrush to drive screws into a wall. It's simply the wrong tool for the job.

undermines the glory of God. They believed that God had to have created each species, from scratch, rather than overseeing a process by which simpler life forms became more complex. The most famous of the battles between Christianity and evolution was played out in a courtroom in Dayton, Tennessee, in July 1925. In March of that year the Tennessee legislature had made it illegal to teach any theory that contradicted the creation of humankind as taught in the Bible. Christian attorney William Jennings Bryan won the case, and high school teacher John Scopes was found guilty of breaking the law. The constitutionality of the law was upheld; it was not repealed until 1967. Bryan may have won the case, but in the realm of public opinion, it was Christianity that lost and appeared to be backward in its thinking. In the latter part of the twentieth century, the battle was on

> **SCIENCE HELPS**
>
> us understand how the
>
> universe works. Faith, on
>
> the other hand, aims to
>
> teach us what our
>
> existence means.

again as fundamentalists challenged textbooks and demanded that creationism be taught alongside evolution.

To many Christians, evolution is simply a way of describing a process that God established for creating the magnificent forms of life we have today. Henry Ford designed the automobile assembly line. He approved the designs of his cars. His name appears on every car. Yet he did not personally build each car. They were his design. His fingerprints were all over the process. Millions of Fords were produced during his watch over the company. No one says that because Ford didn't personally build each car with his own hands he wasn't ultimately responsible for the Ford automobile. If there had been no Henry Ford, there would have been no Ford Automobile Company. Think of creation in this way: God created the processes and the plans for progression of life on our planet. God is still the Creator. Whether each species was individually crafted by God, or the result of a process God designed matters little to me. God remains the Creator either way.

Science and faith are two different ways of understanding our existence. Science helps us understand the physical processes—how the universe works. This is hugely important and, as I've already noted, no threat to genuine faith. Theology and faith, on the other hand, aim to teach us what our existence means. While science asks the questions *what* and *how*, theology seeks to answer the questions *why* and *for what purpose*. Both sets of questions are important.

Can science *by itself* answer questions of ultimate meaning? No. Science isn't equipped or designed to address these questions. A Philips-head screwdriver is a wonderful tool for tightening and loosening screws. But if you need to paint a wall, that screwdriver is just not the right tool for the job. And that's how it is when you try to use science to answer questions of purpose and meaning. It's not going to help because that is not the job it was designed to do. And when we try to use the Bible to answer scientific questions, it's a bit like trying to use a paintbrush to drive screws into a wall. It is the wrong tool for the job.

This is why Christians get it wrong when they

THE CREATION stories in Genesis were not meant to teach us *how* God created, but *that* God created.

treat the book of Genesis as a science textbook. It stands to reason that if you look in the wrong place for something, you are not going to find it. If you pick up a detective novel expecting to find a recipe for cherry pie, you will be disappointed. The same is true if you go looking for "who done it" in a cookbook. So why do many Christians think they will find a scientific explanation of the origins of the universe in a poetic narrative about God the Creator?

The creation stories in Genesis were not meant to teach us *how* God created, but *that* God created. They are written in deliberately dramatic and vivid language; I hear music when I read them. They are meant to stir the soul with the image of God calling forth light from darkness then creating the earth, sun, moon, and stars, all the creatures of the land and sea, and finally human beings themselves. The stories teach us that there *is* a God, that God is good, that creation is a good gift of God, and that human beings are created in God's image (not in our physical appearance, but in our capacity to love, to think, to reason, to make moral decisions, and to act as co-creators with God).

Several years ago, to help our congregation see how science and faith are not enemies but companions in a search for knowledge and truth, I preached a series of sermons titled "Where Science and Religion Meet."[1] We went to area universities, including the University of Kansas and the University of Missouri in Kansas City, and interviewed professors of astrophysics, biology, psychology, and others. We wanted people to see that one does not have to choose between science and faith but that both are valuable partners in understanding our place in the universe. To the surprise of some people, the study of science, far from damaging their faith, actually deepened it.

One young man who joined us for that particular sermon series—watching each sermon online[2]—was an evolutionary biologist and professor at Cornell University named Scott Williamson. Scott's work on recent evolutionary changes in the human genome was chosen as number forty-three of the one hundred most important scientific discoveries of 2007 by *Discover Magazine.* Scott, who considered himself an atheist, was in Kansas City at Christmas and had attended the Christmas Eve service when we announced this sermon series. He was intrigued that a church was willing to approach science and scientists not as enemies, but as colleagues on a quest for truth. He watched each sermon and later wrote to say that, though he had been a lifelong atheist, the sermon series had convinced him that it was possible to be a "scientist and thinking person." He wrote that he had come to believe in the existence of God. He also noted that his wife's love had also played a key role in experiencing the love of God.

> **CHRISTIANS GET**
>
> it right when they see
> science as an important
> companion in the quest for
> knowledge and truth.

Scott was diagnosed with a brain tumor shortly after this and died a year later. Before he died, we had opportunities to e-mail and talk by phone and in person as he was deepening his new-found faith and seeking to understand the significance of the Christian gospel as he approached death.

Scott's story points to the importance of both science and faith. Scott was doing very important work at Cornell in the area of biology—making discoveries that answered the *how* and *what* questions. But he began to long for more. He wanted to know *why* and *for what purpose*. He wanted to know if there was a God who really did know and love him. He wanted to know if he would continue to live after his physical body succumbed to cancer. These were not questions science could answer. As Scott's physical illness progressed, we talked about the resurrection of Jesus and the hope of the biblical authors that this world is not all that there is to existence. I read the words of the apostle Paul to him from 2 Corinthians 4:16–5:1:

So we do not lose heart. Even though our outer nature is wasting away, our inner nature is being renewed day by day. For this slight momentary affliction is preparing us for an eternal weight of glory beyond all measure, because we look not at what can be seen but at what cannot be seen; for what can be seen is temporary, but what cannot be seen is eternal. For we know that if the earthly tent we live in is destroyed, we have a building from God, a house not made with hands, eternal in the heavens.

And we talked about trusting God with our lives and trusting in Christ whose death and resurrection can give us life and hope.

Shortly before Scott's death, he had compasses engraved for his young daughters—he loved hiking with them and he wanted to leave them something that would guide them long after he was gone. On the compasses the engraving read, "I will be with you wherever, whenever, forever." He said to his wife, Shannon, shortly before his death, "I will love you forever." His hope of watching his children even after his death and of loving his wife forever came not from the field of science but from his newfound faith.

Christians get it wrong when they see science as a threat to faith, or when they try to make the Bible a scientific textbook. But they get it right when they see science as an important companion in the quest for knowledge and truth.

POSTSCRIPT: POLITICS AND RELIGION

Let's consider another area where young people believe Christians get it wrong. I recently received an e-mail from a young woman in response to my request for stories of when Christians get it wrong. She told me that she had not grown up in church, but that in recent months she had become a Christian and joined a church. She also said that she was a Democrat, and that when she became a Christian she thought that her political beliefs on issues like poverty, education, the environment, and health care were a good fit for her Christian convictions on compassion and care of others. But that's not what some of the folks at her church thought. She came away from conversations with them sensing that they believed that her political and social views were inconsistent with her newfound faith. More than one person implied that she couldn't be both a Christian and a Democrat.

This young adult, who has recently joined the faith, was essentially being told that her

> **WHEN IT** comes to politics, some Christians say and do things in the name of God that are the antithesis of the gospel.

kind wasn't welcome in the church she had just joined and that her political views might keep her out of heaven. I wondered what kind of church would say such things. Aren't committed and idealistic young folks like her precisely the sort of people churches should be reaching out to? I wrote to ask her what church she belonged to where some Christians said this to her. To my surprise and disappointment she said that she had joined the church I pastor!

I pastor a church in a predominantly "red" state, yet our congregation is divided between Democrats and Republicans. We have leaders and elected officials from both parties, including our state's Democratic Governor and several Republican legislators. I appreciate some elements of both parties and disagree with others. I have voted for persons in both parties. I am convinced that Jesus would not perfectly fit either of them. But I think the way Christians sometimes engage in politics has been damaging, particularly for many young adults. I received the following note from one of our older parishioners when I asked about how Christians get it wrong in politics:

> Your question caused a rush of memories of our most recent national political campaign. We have a number of very close friends who are passionate about their politics. They regularly profess their strong Christian commitments, but somehow have a blind spot when it comes to how they react to views and opinions of

those with whom they differ. . . .When we get close to that political arena, I have trouble sensing any Christian love or tolerance of any perspective but their own.

But it is deeper than attitude and opinions. Some Christians, in the name of God, say and do things in the realm of politics that are the antithesis of the gospel: slander, gossip, malicious talk, mean-spirited rhetoric, disrespect, and worse. This has been particularly true when it comes to spreading rumors and half-truths using the Internet. I am disappointed at how often Christians I know forward slanderous e-mail to everyone on their e-mail list without taking the time to verify the claims in the message. It doesn't matter whether you are a Democrat or a Republican, you have a moral and spiritual responsibility not to slander or send out inflammatory e-mails about the opposing party or its candidates.

The apostle Paul offers instructions for Christians to conduct themselves in all areas of life. These words are particularly pertinent when it comes to politics:

> Let no evil talk come out of your mouths, but only what is useful for building up, as there is need, so that your words may give grace to those who hear. And do not grieve the Holy Spirit of God. . . . Put away from you all bitterness and wrath and anger and wrangling and slander, together with all malice, and be kind to one another. (Ephesians 4:29-32)

Paul notes that when we act in belligerent ways we "grieve the Holy Spirit of God." The Greek word for *grieve* means to "inflict distress or intense sadness upon." That is what Christians

CHRISTIANS GET

it wrong in the area of politics when they too closely associate their faith with a political party, or engage in slander and mean-spirited partisan attacks.

do to God when they speak words that tear others down, or that slander them. Christians are called to speak words that "give grace"—that is, undeserved kindness—to all.

Christians should be engaged in the political arena. I encourage our church members to consider civil service as a calling. But Christians get it wrong in the area of politics when they too closely associate their faith with a political party, or they lay aside Christian ethics and Christ's call to love even our enemies, and instead they engage in slander and mean-spirited partisan politics. Christians get it right when they work for justice, and when grace, truth, and love mark their political activities.

NOTES

1. This series of sermons is available on audio CD or DVD at http://thewell.cor.org.

2. Our worship services are streamed every weekend and the sermons are posted for free download as podcasts or can be viewed online. Visit our Web site at http://www.cor.org.

CHAPTER 3

WHEN SPEAKING
OF OTHER
RELIGIONS

Growing up in a suburb of Kansas City in the 1960s and 1970s, I didn't know any Muslims, Hindus, or Buddhists. My sole exposure to people of other faiths was one Jewish friend. At that time, most Kansas City country clubs did not allow Jewish members, and a number of communities, including the one where the church

JOHN SAID,

"You're going to tell me that this person who lived a . . . life of straight moral value is going to go to hell just because he didn't say 'I love Jesus'? There's something there that is not right."

I serve is located, carried deed restrictions prohibiting Jews from buying homes. It was unthinkable that a Muslim or Hindu or Buddhist might move into the neighborhood. Who determined that Jews and other religious groups should not be allowed to move into these communities or join the country clubs?

It was much easier in those days to unquestioningly accept the assumptions that people of other faiths were ignorant and misguided heathens and that they would, on Judgment Day, be consigned to hell for not having chosen the one true religion.

Fast-forward forty years. It is unthinkable that people of non-Christian religions would be prohibited from buying homes in certain neighborhoods or joining certain country clubs. If you live in an urban area, it is likely that you have at least one friend, coworker, or neighbor who is practicing a faith other than Christian. For many Christians, the more people they know who are devout members of other religions the harder it becomes to believe that all such people will suffer eternally in hell because they did not call upon the name of Jesus Christ. This is particularly true for young adults who have grown up in a more multicultural, pluralistic world than previous generations.

During his six years of service in Afghanistan and Iraq, John had been surrounded by men, women, and children who were raised in a world that is as Muslim as the United States is thought to be Christian. He saw people stop what they were doing in the middle of the day and fall to their knees in prayer; he saw their devotion to God and observed their efforts to faithfully live their scriptures. John became increasingly skeptical of Christian claims about the fate of people of other religions. In our meeting together, this is what he said about how Christians get it wrong regarding people of other faiths:

> One of the things I have always had trouble swallowing with the Christian faith is that we have a God of compassion, a God of love, a God of forgiveness, but if you don't say "Jesus you're my savior," you're gonna burn. Flat out. . . . That's not forgiving, that's not compassion, that's coercion, that's blackmail. People all over the world . . . could live the best life. They could be compassionate, they could be understanding, they could do their best to help their community, to help other people, to serve their nation . . . but you're going to tell me that

this person who lived an idyllic life of straight moral value is going to go to hell just because he didn't say "I love Jesus"? There's something there that is not right. There is something about that puzzle piece that doesn't fit in with what Christian faith is trying to sell.

Let's look at how Christians get it wrong regarding the theological question of the eternal fate of people of other religions, and what it might look like when Christians get it right.

CHRISTIANITY THAT REPELS

Let's clarify for a moment what we mean by people of "other faiths." In this chapter, I mean people who are adherents of a religion other than Christian. Orthodox Christians, Roman Catholics, and Protestants all claim to be followers of Jesus Christ. They represent different sects within the Christian faith. For our purposes here, "other faiths" refers to Jews, Muslims, Hindus, Buddhists, and others.

THE PROBLEM comes when Christians share their faith in ways that are arrogant, disrespectful, hurtful, insulting, or insensitive.

Most Amer-icans know very little about faiths other than their own. How much do you know about Islam, Hinduism, Buddhism, or Judaism? Here's a little pop quiz to test your knowledge:

- When do most Jews gather for worship (what day of the week and what portion of the day)?
- In what century did Mohammed die?
- Name the one Hindu scripture that is likely to be in every Hindu's home.
- When did the Buddha live?

In an informal survey of my Christian friends, few were able to answer more than one of these questions correctly.*

When my older daughter was sixteen, she came to me and said, "Dad, I'm a Christian because you are a Christian. I've not studied any of the other world religions. I don't know anything about them. How can I

---

* (1) Most Jews gather on Friday evenings for worship—the Jewish Sabbath runs from sunset Friday to sunset Saturday. (2) Mohammed lived from 570 to 632 CE. (3) Most Hindu homes have a copy of the Bhagavad-Gita. (4) Scholars are not certain when the Buddha lived, but there is consensus that he lived 700 to 900 years after the time of Moses and 400 to 500 years before the time of Jesus. His teachings were committed to writing about the time Jesus lived.

SURPRISINGLY,

I found my own Christian

faith deepened by this

study of other religions.

know that Christianity is true if I've not considered any of the other faiths?" Danielle was reflecting the sentiments of many young adults today.

Her question gave me an idea. What would happen if I could lead my entire congregation in a study of four of the great religions of the world—Hinduism, Buddhism, Islam, Judaism—and then compare and contrast them with Christianity in a way that demonstrated respect and humility while honestly examining the differences between them? I spent six months preparing for this sermon series. I read the Koran, portions of the Hindu Vedas, and selections from various Buddhist writings. I interviewed leading individuals representing each of these faiths and attended their worship services and rituals. Then I announced to our congregation that I would be leading this study. Most people were excited, but some people worried that if I preached this series of sermons people might lose their faith. Some, I think, were worried about losing their *own* faith.

Surprisingly, I found my own Christian faith deepened by this study. As I gained understanding and appreciation for what others believe and why, my convictions about the Christian faith grew stronger. At the same time, the other faiths challenged me to be a better Christian. For instance, Muslims pray five times a day and give 2.5 percent of their income to the needy. My study of Islam led me to spend more time in prayer and to a deeper desire to give to the poor. The Hindu philosophy of non-injury helped me see love in new ways. The Buddha's existential struggles related to suffering and death gave me a deeper appreciation for the Christian doctrines of redemption and resurrection.

Several dozen people actually left our church, unsettled by these sermons, but several *hundred* people chose to become Christians after hearing how we approached these other faiths with respect and a willingness to learn from them, while honestly pointing out our differences. In addition, the entire congregation came to better understand their Muslim, Hindu, Buddhist, and Jewish friends, and we are able to talk with them with respect and appreciation.[1]

Some Christians take a very different approach to talking about other religions. A

> **PRESSURE TO** accept Christ seldom leads to a desire to become a Christian. No one enjoys a high-pressure sales job.

young woman wrote and described her of Christians sharing their faith while she was in college:

> My college roommate and I were invited to a party being put on by a Christian group. The party was fun, and when they invited us to their Bible study later that week, we both said sure. The Bible study was anything but fun. Almost from the start, the discussion centered on whether Jews would get to heaven. No one in the group thought they would. In fact, several in the group spoke as though the Jews were responsible for killing Jesus. My friend finally spoke up and told them that she was Jewish. The study went downhill from there. Some were soft sell, some hard sell, but all of them tried to convince my friend to "ask Jesus into her heart." When we left that evening, I'm not sure who was more upset, her or me. Since that night I haven't had anything to do with Christians.

Pressure to accept Christ seldom leads to a desire to become a Christian. No one enjoys a high-pressure sales job. When I spoke with John, he described his feelings about Christians seeking to pressure him into becoming a Christian:

> The one thing that will set me and so many other people right on their heels is when Christians are intrusive. It's when you really start pushing for it, you know. If you are going to [help a nonbeliever find faith] it's not something they're going to come to in one conversation, so do not try to convert people in one fell swoop. You might get 1 in 100, but you're going to drive the other 99 the hell away.

There is nothing wrong with Christians sharing their faith. Jesus spoke of his message as good news—and good news should be shared. The prob-

NOT ALL

Christians throughout history have held the view that non-Christians would spend eternity in hell.

lem is when Christians share their faith in ways that are arrogant, disrespectful, hurtful, insulting, or insensitive.

In the first century of the Christian era, Christians were a tiny minority within the Roman Empire, when most people believed in a variety of gods. Today's Christians would do well to recall how the apostles instructed early Christians to live their lives and to share their faith. The apostle Paul, in Acts 17, speaks to a group of Greek philosophers in Athens. He doesn't insult them. He looks for common ground with them. He quotes their poets. He even identifies one of the unknown gods they worship with the God of the Bible. The apostle Peter, in his first letter, offers the following counsel to Christians on how they might share their faith: "live such good lives among the pagans that . . . they may see your good deeds" (2:12 NIV). He told them to "show proper respect to everyone" (v. 17). He tells them to carry themselves with humility noting, "God opposes the proud but gives grace to the humble" (5:5). And he says, "Be compassionate and humble. . . . Always be prepared to give an answer to everyone who asks you to give the reason for the hope that you have. But do this with *gentleness and respect*" (3:8, 15; emphasis added).

The Christians in the college Bible study felt great urgency to lead the young Jewish woman to accept Christ. The urgency and the pressure they applied had something to do with their belief that if the young woman did not accept Christ then she would spend eternity in hell. They were certain that this fate awaits anyone who has not accepted Jesus Christ. Will God welcome to heaven only those who call upon the name of Jesus, regardless of those persons' character, actions, or actual love of God and neighbor? To young adults, this idea is unthinkable. They find it inconsistent with a God of justice, mercy, and love.

THE FATE OF FAITHFUL, PRACTICING JEWS, MUSLIMS, AND HINDUS

Let's consider three distinct answers Christians give to the question, What is the fate of faithful, practicing Jews, Muslims, and Hindus? I mention these three groups because, in the case of Muslims and Hindus, they are the next two largest religious groups in the world, following Christianity. I mention Jews because Christians are most likely to know practicing Jews. Further I am specifically speaking of persons who seek to know, love, and serve God as they have been taught about God by their religions.

CHRISTIAN EXCLUSIVISM

Christians from the conservative and evangelical traditions typically answer the question of the eternal fate of faithful Jews, Muslims, and Hindus in a way similar to what we have considered so far—such persons will be damned because they did not avail themselves of the gift of salvation offered in Jesus Christ. According to this view, human beings are born contaminated by sin. Sin separates us from God both here on earth and in eternity. A holy and righteous God cannot admit persons who are still sinful into heaven. God has provided, by the offering of his Son, salvation from sin and death. It is available to all. But one has to take hold of this salvation by trusting in Christ. Imagine a person drowning in the sea. A life preserver is tossed

IN ITS harshest form this view excludes from heaven any who have never heard the good news of Jesus Christ.

from a ship. The person must still take hold of the life preserver to be saved from drowning. Jesus Christ is the life preserver offered by God to all. In rejecting the life preserver, the individual is left to save herself or himself—a feat that is said to be impossible for human beings.

In the fifth century, Saint Augustine championed this view. It was restated by John Calvin in the sixteenth century. In its harshest, yet most consistent form, it excludes from heaven even infants who die who did not receive Christ. It excludes those with mental disabilities who do not receive Christ. It excludes from heaven any who have never heard the good news of Jesus Christ. Many Christians allow exceptions in these cases, but the most consistent and hard-line do not.

I spoke with an individual who holds the hard-line, exclusivist view on this issue. He was leaving our church because of the sermons I was preaching on different religions. I asked, "Are you suggesting that the Native Americans who lived on this continent for thousands of years before the first missionaries arrived were all sent to hell even though they never had the opportunity to hear of Jesus Christ? We know many of them were deeply religious and sought God. Regardless of how they lived, how much they sought God, all of them—every man, woman, and child—was destined for hell without any opportunity to even call upon the name of Jesus Christ?"

He responded that this was correct, that God could have revealed his Son to them in some other way, but barring that, they were in hell.

It should be said that many evangelical Christians find the hard-line position difficult to accept; they allow exceptions. They speak of an "age of accountability" for children, before which, if they die, they are received into heaven. They say that mentally handicapped people will be judged based upon what they can understand of the grace of God. Some are willing to say the same of persons who have never heard the name of Christ. These persons will be judged based upon how they respond to God's grace as they are able to know and understand it.

CHRISTIAN UNIVERSALISM

A second answer to the question of the fate of faithful Jews, Muslims, and Hindus is the absolute opposite of Exclusivism. It is called *Christian Universalism* (not to be confused with the Unitarian Universalist denomination). This view suggests that all persons—not just faithful Jews, Muslims, and Hindus but all persons—will ultimately be reconciled to God and are bound for the kingdom of Heaven. Christians who hold this view, who also believe in hell, think of hell as a temporary place with the primary focus of redemption rather than punishment. Hell's purpose is to lead people

FOR THOSE

who don't understand or have not made sense of the gospel, but who have sought God, this very act of seeking God is an expression of faith.

to repentance. Supporters of Christian Universalism claim that many of the most important theologians of the early church held this view.[2]

I like this idea, and it solves several theological problems. The challenge it poses for me is that it appears to remove human freedom to reject God, at least in the ultimate sense. The Bible teaches that God has given human beings the freedom to resist God's grace, to reject God's will, and to do what God finds abhorrent (the most obvious examples being the totalitarian dictators like Hitler, Stalin, Pol Pot, and a host of others who made themselves out to be gods and who were responsible for the murder of millions of human beings).

CHRISTIAN INCLUSIVISM

Christian Inclusivism offers a third alternative. It teaches that Jesus is the Son of God. That he came to offer salvation for the world. It teaches that the salvation of the human race is made possible by Jesus Christ. But this salvation can be given by God regardless of whether an individual personally knows Jesus Christ. God can offer this gift based upon the criteria God chooses.

This view also notes that the Christian gospel teaches that salvation is a gift given by God. Human beings do nothing to merit salvation; we simply trust in it. We receive it as a gift of God's grace. Our part is simply faith. The question, as it pertains to faithful adherents of other religions, is do they have faith? They may not have complete knowledge of what God has done in Jesus Christ, but they can nevertheless have complete trust in God. The view offers as evidence that those in the Bible who came before the time of Jesus also were saved by faith—faith that did not include Jesus Christ, for he had not yet been born (see Hebrews 11:4-40).

Inclusivism reminds us that the Christian gospel, the good news, is that we are saved by grace. In the New Testament, grace refers to God's kindness, love, care, work on our behalf, blessings, gifts, goodness, and

> **WE ARE**
>
> saved by *God's* initiative, because of *God's* love, *God's* righteousness, *God's* kindness, and *God's* mercy.

salvation. But it is more than that—it is *undeserved*. God's grace is pure gift.

The apostle Paul lays out the Christian conception of how salvation works in Ephesians 2:4-5, 8-9:

> God, who is rich in mercy, out of the great love with which he loved us even when we were dead through our trespasses, made us alive together with Christ. . . . For by grace you have been saved through faith, and this is not your own doing; it is the gift of God—not the result of works, so that no one may boast.

We are saved by *God's* initiative, because of *God's* love, *God's* righteousness, *God's* kindness, and *God's* mercy. For those who don't understand or have not made sense of the gospel, but who have sought God—to love God, to do what God desires—the very act of seeking God is an expression of faith.

Many conservative and evangelical Christians are surprised to hear that evangelical thinker C. S. Lewis seems to have held this view. It was powerfully laid out in the last of his series of children's books, *The Chronicles of Narnia*. Near the end of *The Last Battle*, we find what many interpret as a mythical portrayal of Judgment Day. Jesus is portrayed as the lion, Aslan. A man is being brought before him for judgment. The man, Emeth, has spent his entire life following the false god, Tash. He was raised by his parents to worship and serve Tash. As

Emeth sees Aslan the Lion, he suddenly realizes that Tash was not god. He falls to his face, preparing for his own destruction. Here is how Emeth describes what happens next:

> He touched my forehead . . . and said, Son, thou art welcome. But I said, Alas, Lord, I am no son of thine but the servant of Tash. He answered, Child, all the service thou hast done to Tash, I account as service done to me." . . . Then I said, "Lord, is it then true . . . that thou and Tash are one?" The Lion growled. . . . "It is false." I said, . . . "I have been seeking Tash all my days." "Beloved," said the Glorious One, "unless thy desire had been for me thou wouldst not have sought so long and so truly. For all find what they truly seek."[3]

A number of prominent Christians have held this view—with varying shades and gradations—including Justin Martyr in the early church, John Wesley, the founder of the Methodist movement, evangelical theologian John Stott, and most recently Billy Graham. Inclusivism is also the official position of the Roman Catholic Church and the generally accepted view of most mainline Protestants.

This is also my own view of how God will judge non-Christians who earnestly seek to know, love, and follow God in the ways they are taught. This view maintains that salvation is by and through Christ, and that it is received by faith. It makes clear that salvation is a gift

I TELL others about Jesus, not because I'm afraid God will eternally torment them in hell if I don't, but because I believe that in him we see God.

from God, given not based upon human actions, nor even as a result of our theological knowledge. It is given by God, through Christ, to whomever God wishes to give it. Based upon the Gospel accounts of Jesus' ministry, God seems to desire to give salvation to all who would listen and trust in his mercy.

When I think about God's mercy toward humankind, I'm reminded of a hymn written in 1854 by Frederic Farber, "There's a Wideness in God's Mercy":

> There's a wideness in God's mercy
> like the wideness of the sea;
> there's a kindness in God's justice,
> which is more than liberty.
>
> There is welcome for the sinner,
> and more graces for the good!
> There is mercy with the Savior,
> there is healing in his blood.

For the love of God is broader
than the measure of our mind;
and the heart of the Eternal
is most wonderfully kind.

THEN WHY SHARE THE GOSPEL?

Whenever I share this idea of Christian Inclusivism, someone inevitably asks, "Then why should we bother to share the gospel with people, if God may save them anyway? Why have so many missionaries risked their lives to offer Christ to people who did not know him?" I usually respond with several questions of my own: Do you mean to suggest that the only reason we share the good news of Jesus Christ is that we believe God will eternally torment people in hell if we don't tell them about Jesus? Is avoiding hell the only reason to become a Christian? Is Christianity really only about getting a ticket to heaven?

I tell others about Jesus Christ not because I'm afraid God will eternally torment them in hell if I don't persuade them to accept Christ; I share Jesus Christ with others because I believe that in him we see and understand who God is and who we are meant to be. I share Christ with others because I believe he teaches us about the love, mercy, and grace of God. From him we learn sacrificial love. In him we experience forgiveness and mercy. I tell others about Christ because I believe he is the way, the truth, and the life. I tell others about Christ because he has changed my life so that the richest and most meaningful parts of my life are somehow made so by him. I share Christ with others because I want them to know that God already loves them, and that Christ offers us both the truth about God and God's will for humanity. I share Christ with others because in Christ we hear the good news of God's sacrificial love, of forgiveness of sins, and of the hope of everlasting life. But I do not share Christ because I believe God eternally torments those who love him but don't understand to call upon the name of Christ.

WHEN CHRISTIANS GET IT RIGHT

A number of persons at the church that I serve were once Hindus, Buddhists, Muslims, or Jews who have become followers of Jesus Christ. They became followers of Jesus not because we pressured them into accepting Christ. They became followers of Jesus Christ not because we spoke ill of their former faith. And they became Christians not because we made them feel small if they did not become Christians. Instead most of our members demonstrate respect, humility, and love. At their best, our members seek to listen to and learn from people of other faiths while humbly sharing their own faith.

Ali and his wife, Fay, began attending our church in 1996. Fay was a Christian; Ali was a Muslim. A very bright man, Ali had a successful career before retiring. He attended church every Sunday with his wife because he loved her, and she loved going to church. He even volunteered each week on our bulletin-stuffing team. The people in our 7:45 a.m. service knew that Ali was a Muslim, but that did not stop them from welcoming him with open arms, inviting him to Sunday school and to join them in serving. They never pressured him to accept Christ. They listened and showed respect for his faith while humbly sharing their own.

Four years ago Fay died. I officiated at her funeral. I worried that once Fay was gone Ali might no longer attend church. But the Sunday after her funeral there he was, sitting in his normal seat. Last year Ali moved to Florida to be closer to his son. After his move he sent me an e-mail:

> Adam, I always believed in one God. Now I believe Jesus was the Son of God. I have been a very religious person in my life, but somehow I did not fit any one label. I do not like it when people push their religion on me. You never did. You accepted me as I am.

I sought to demonstrate this acceptance, love, and respect to Ali, but it was the people in worship, at Sunday school, and on the Friday bulletin-stuffing team who accepted and loved Ali.

When Christians get it right, they show respect for people of other faiths. They listen to them, learn from them, and humbly share their faith with them. They look for points of contact and commonality, as Paul did with the philosophers in Athens. They offer reasons for their faith in Jesus Christ with gentleness and respect, as Peter taught.

NOTES

1. This series was later published as a book and video-based small-group study, *Christianity and World Religions* (Nashville: Abingdon Press, 2005).

2. See http://www.tentmaker.org/tracts/Universalists.html, which includes Clement of Alexandria, Origen, Athanasius, Ambrose, John Chrysostom, Eusebius, Gregory of Nyssa, and Jerome among those who held the Universalist view.

3. C. S. Lewis, *The Last Battle* (New York: HarperCollins, 1956/1984), 186–87.

CHAPTER 4

··

WHEN BAD
THINGS HAPPEN

The greatest challenge to faith in God for many people is reconciling a loving God with the suffering and pain they see in the world around them. When I talked with John, the young Army Airborne Ranger who had just returned from Iraq, he described losing five of his friends in battle. Then he said, "Over the years I've looked back and I just

SOME MAY find comfort in the idea that God brings about the death of six-week-old children, but most would find it difficult to worship, love, serve, and trust a God who acts in this way.

remember thinking, you know, if there's a God that's loving and compassionate, then why did he kill John? When someone tells you that there's a God, he loves you, and he cares about you, and he has a plan for you—how the hell did that plan factor in when he killed five of my friends?"

This is a serious theological question—how can a good and loving God allow, or perhaps even cause, the suffering that happens in our world? Theologians speak of this as the "problem of evil" and give the line of questioning a name: *theodicy* (from the Greek *theo*—God and *dike*—justice). Every theologian and every thoughtful Christian will wrestle with this question. The purpose of this chapter is not to provide *the* answer to the question—though I'll suggest a line of reasoning that may be helpful. I would like to suggest that the long and commonly held assumptions about God's involvement in the affairs of our world—the things Christians say in the face of suffering, and even in the face of blessing—may be both wrong and actually serve to push people away from God. I invite Christians and non-Christians alike to question the assumptions you may have been taught regarding God's relationship to both the evil and the good that happens in our world and to ultimately get it right when it comes to how we speak about God and suffering.

DOES EVERYTHING HAPPEN FOR A REASON?

As I mentioned previously, a couple of years ago our church set up a blog inviting young adults to respond to the question, *When do Christians get it wrong?* One young woman posted this reply:

> Our baby died this past spring when he was six weeks old. So many Christians we have encountered since that time tell us "this was God's plan." . . . Before this tragic event, I guess I thought this was how life worked too. . . . But there is no way that the death of an innocent six-week-old and our inability to get pregnant again is part of some master plan. And if it

CHRISTIANS REALLY get it wrong when they begin to diagnose the suffering of others as acts of God's judgment.

is then I'm simply not interested in the God that has that plan.

Well-meaning Christians, seeking to offer comfort to this woman, had the opposite impact. They neither comforted her, nor helped her draw comfort from God. Instead, they implied that God was responsible for the death of this woman's baby. Some may find comfort in the idea that God brings about the death of six-week-old children, but most would find it difficult to worship, love, serve, and trust a God who acts in this way.

Christians often say things like "It must be the will of God" or "Everything happens for a reason." The former assumes that everything happens because God wills it to happen. The latter assumes that God has a plan in place—a predetermined script for our planet and everyone on it—and that everything that happens is written in the script and serves a purpose that we simply cannot see right now. Most people accept these assumptions without question. I invite you to question them. (At the end of this chapter I will suggest that God does have a plan, but that it may be broader than we can imagine.)

The young woman's friends sought to console her by saying that the death of her child was part of God's plan. It is unlikely that their intention was to associate her suffering with God's punishment or judgment, although that is often what we tend to do in regard to the suffering of another. Individuals going through adversity may also believe that God is punishing them. As I was talking with a man who had lost his job in the "Great Recession" of 2008–2009, he asked, "What have I done that was so bad that God is punishing me like this?" The man assumed that his job loss was God's doing, and when he could not find another job, his mind immediately moved to the idea of punishment.

Part of what this man needed was for someone to help him question his original assumption. Did the entire U.S. economy falter simply so God could punish this one man? Were all of the people who were laid off in need of God's punishment? Did God cause the economic recession that led to the loss of his job? Or was this the result of a lot of very bad economic decisions made on the part of people on both Wall Street and Main Street? These questions needed to be explored with this man.

It is worth questioning when an individual believes that some act of suffering is God's punishment. Christians really get it wrong, however, when

THIS CHRISTIAN was certain that God had brought Katrina to punish the heathens of New Orleans, Alabama, and Mississippi.

they begin to tell others that their suffering is God's judgment.

In August 2005, Hurricane Katrina struck the Gulf Coast of the United States causing the death of more than eighteen hundred people and tens of thousands of people to lose their homes. Following the hurricane, I recall reading one man's blog about the destruction of so much of the Gulf Coast:

> Many thoughtful Americans are asking, "Why did this happen?" There is an answer to this question. . . . The answer is found in understanding that man is not in control. God is! Everything in the sky, the sea and on earth is subject to His control. . . . Was there wickedness in New Orleans, Alabama and Mississippi? Well, let's see. There was the burgeoning Gulf Coast gambling industry, with a new casino that was to open on Labor Day weekend. . . . And then there was the 34th Annual gay, lesbian and transgender . . . Labor Day gala. . . . Further, there is the well-known corruption, drugs, and immoral playground of the French Quarter.

This Christian was very clear—God sent the hurricane as an act of judgment upon the sin prevalent on the Gulf Coast. Never mind that the "immoral playground of the French Quarter" was actually spared by Katrina! Never mind that the casinos along the Gulf Coast reported their best year ever the year after they reopened. And never mind that there were thousands of Christians who lost their homes and some their lives in the destruction! This

Christian was certain that God had brought Katrina to punish the heathens of New Orleans, Alabama, and Mississippi!

People of faith have struggled with viewing suffering as God's judgment since biblical times. This is how much of the Old Testament views suffering. If you suffer, it is because you have sinned. But in the middle of the Old Testament is a book that was written to counter this idea. The book of Job is the story of a man who is righteous, and yet he suffers greatly. His friends arrive to comfort him, and at first they do a wonderful job. Here's how the book describes the scene when they first come to be with their friend:

> Now when Job's three friends heard of all these troubles that had come upon him, each of them set out from his home—Eliphaz the Temanite, Bildad the Shuhite, and Zophar the Naamathite. They met together to go and console and comfort him. When they saw him from a distance, they did not recognize him, and they raised their voices and wept aloud; they tore their robes and threw dust in the air upon their heads. They sat with him on the ground seven days and seven nights, and no one spoke a word to him, for they saw that his suffering was very great. (Job 2:11-13)

Here his friends do what friends need to do. They just sit in silence with him. They don't try to explain anything. They don't think that something they say is going to make things better. They don't presume to have all the

WHEN CHRISTIANS begin to suggest that suffering is God's punishment for sin, I wonder if they are not in some sense negating the cross of Christ.

answers; they just sit with him in silence and grieve with him.

But then after seven days of sitting with Job, his friends make their big mistake —they begin opening their mouths! And as they do, they begin to tell Job that his suffering must be his fault, that it is the judgment of God, and that he should repent. Job continues to maintain his innocence. The book ends with God chastising Job's friends and blessing Job. It provides little explanation of Job's suffering except to make the point that it was not punishment for something Job had done wrong.

Everything changes in the New Testament, where we find Jesus suffering for the sins of the world. Whatever suffering our collective sin might merit, Jesus bears it for humankind. When Christians begin to suggest that suffering is God's punishment for sin, I wonder if they are not in some sense negating the cross of Christ.

Now there is sometimes a connection between sin and suffering. But the connection is not God handing down punishment. As I read the New Testament, our punishment was taken by Jesus on the cross. When we sin, there are consequences, however. *Sin* signifies turning from God's intention for our lives; the Greek word *hamartia* was a term from archery that meant, among other things, to "miss the mark." The consequences are not punishments from God; they are the natural result of doing the wrong thing. When we cheat on our spouses, pain results. When we are caught in a lie, we lose the trust of others and we experience shame. These are natural consequences of doing the wrong thing. But Christians who evaluate the suffering of others and pronounce that it is a result of the other's sin are getting it wrong. In fact, to do so is a sin.

GOD THE MICROMANAGER?

Let's return to the assumption that everything happens according to the will of God.

Christians who believe that God is controlling everything often speak of God's "sovereignty." This term means that God is the highest authority, there is no one to whom God reports and no one to whom God answers. God is the Supreme Ruler—the "King of the Universe." The universe is the rightful property of God, who created it. Nearly all Christians would agree that God is sovereign—the highest authority and not dependent

> ## DOES GOD
>
> control each cell, all the time, in every one of the earth's six billion people? Does God determine at any given moment that a particular cell in this person should die, or that this cell should become cancerous?

upon anyone or anything else.

In an attempt to glorify God, however, some people go too far. They claim that God is not only the highest authority but also the "Supreme Micromanager." They would never use this phrase to describe God, but this is what their picture of God looks like. They suggest that God is actually controlling every dimension of creation. This is sometimes referred to as "determinism." The logical outcome of this line of reasoning, as we will see, makes God a monster. Let's consider what it would mean to assume that God controls every dimension of creation.

There are approximately 75 trillion to 100 trillion cells in your body. Does God control each cell, all the time, in every one of the earth's six billion people? Does God determine at any given moment that a particular cell in this person should die, or that this cell should become cancerous? Does God determine every electrical impulse in the body and every thought in every human brain at every moment in order to control every detail of human existence? This is what would be required if God controls all of the affairs of our world.

But it doesn't stop there. In order for God to control everything, God would also need to control the billions and trillions of cells and the brain impulses in all of the trillions of other creatures on our planet; for all of creation is interconnected. Where does this stop? Does God control the properties of every molecule, atom, and electron of everything in creation at all times, dictating that this one should act this way and that one in that way? This is the only way that God could exert complete control over all things at all times in order to ensure that every event happens according to God's will. Those who define sovereignty in terms of control would need to expand God's control beyond our planet to the universe—all 150 billion galaxies like our own Milky Way and the hundreds of billions of stars like our sun that make up each of the 150 billion galaxies in our universe. On each of these and everything in between, God would control every subatomic particle at all times.

This seems a tall order, even for God. I don't suggest that God cannot do this. I believe all creation is sustained by God and draws its existence from God. But if God does exercise this kind of control, it raises a host of

questions. The first is simply, why? Why would God create a universe that requires constant, moment-by-
moment control? Why would God create human beings
with the appearance of freedom and a longing for freedom if God is going to control every thought, every
word, and every action behind the scenes? And if God
controls everything we do, which implies that God also
determines the outcome of all things, what is the point of
exerting any effort? *"Que sera, sera*—what will be,
will be."

This leads to another assumption—that history
unfolds according to God's predetermined plan.
According to this view, God has written a story for the
universe—and for each of us—that is now unfolding.
We don't know how the story goes or how it ends, but
God knows because God wrote the script. We have the
illusion of making our own choices, but in fact we do
no such thing because God has predetermined exactly
what will happen, and we cannot change it. God controls all of the variables so that each person's story pro-
ceeds exactly as God intends.

This raises even more questions. For example: If God
has already decided who will win the Super Bowl, and
the winning and losing teams can do nothing to change
the outcome, why practice, work out, or exert effort to be
better prepared than one's opponent? Whatever you do

you are supposed to do—any choice you make, good or evil, must be the choice God wants you to make. *"Que sera, sera."*

Some people who hold these views will read this chapter and label my views heretical. If that's you, remember that, according to your own views, my writing these words must have been God's plan. According to this view, I didn't strike any of the keys on my computer keyboard of my own volition; it was the impulse of God that led me to say each of these things. So you might want to take up your argument with God. I say that in jest, but the fact is that human responsibility seems to disappear if everything we do is really ultimately what God predetermined before we were born. I have read many arguments that human beings are responsible for their actions despite the fact that God has predetermined what we will do. Personally, I have not found these arguments for determinism completely coherent.

I'm reminded of a character played by comedian Flip Wilson on television in

> TO SAY
>
> that God plans, wills, and prompts the hearts of those who commit heinous crimes in order to accomplish some greater good strikes me as the worst kind of blasphemy.

the 1970s—the character's name was Geraldine—whose favorite phrase was "The devil made me do it." This excused Geraldine from responsibility for any wrongdoing. For hardcore preachers of determinism, the more accurate phrase would be "God made me do it."

Most people become deeply troubled by this picture of God controlling everything when they encounter horrific evil. Some years ago two drug addicts, a man and a woman, went on a rampage, videotaping their rape and murder of a number of women. They kidnapped and brutally tortured a young woman who survived the ordeal. If God has a predetermined plan for each person, and if God controls all things so that everything happens according to God's plan, then these two persons were simply doing what God foreordained. How can this be? How could a loving, just, merciful, and compassionate God plan and will this kind of evil? One might argue, "You haven't seen the tremendous good that will come of such evil. You will be able to see it one day." I believe God is able to redeem suffering and bring good from evil; but to say that God planned, willed, and prompted the hearts of those who committed such a heinous crime in order to accomplish some greater good strikes me as the worst kind of blasphemy. No ends could justify such terrible means. To claim such an act is the will of God is to say that God is neither loving nor just.

We can apply this same line of theological reasoning to every area of life, which means that every automobile accident; every epidemic outbreak; every tornado, hurricane, or earthquake; every act of corporate malfeasance; and every act of human treachery are ultimately scripted by God and occur under God's guiding hand.

I encourage you to question these assumptions about God.

I do not believe God is a micromanager or that everything happens because God wills it. In fact, one overarching message of the Bible for me is that much of what happens in the world is *not* God's will. From the Bible's opening story of Adam and Eve eating the forbidden fruit to its closing story of the forces of darkness waging war against God at Armageddon, human beings are repeatedly guilty of doing the opposite of what God commands.

GIVING GOD CREDIT FOR THE GOOD BUT NOT BLAMING GOD FOR THE BAD?

Some reading this might ask: "If you say that God is not responsible for the bad things that happen, why give God credit for the good things that happen?" This is a great question. How can Christians credit God for the

DOES GOD provide front row parking spaces for some while thousands of others die each day in automobile accidents?

good things while saying that God is not also responsible for the bad? If God is not responsible for the bad things that happen in life, why should we say that God is responsible for the good things?"

These are important questions. Let's consider examples that help illustrate the theological problem and why the language of many Christians, even when it comes to the good things, can turn thinking people away from God.

A wide receiver scores a touchdown in an NFL game and then points to the heavens and makes the sign of the cross. What is the message? If the player is saying, "God, I recognize that you are the source of my life, and I am grateful for you and the opportunities I have and I wish to honor you," that's okay. But if he is pausing to suggest that God orchestrated the touchdown, we would do well to question this line of reasoning. Is God the "12th Man" on the field, playing with whichever team God favors? What does that mean for the other team? Does God help one team or another win? Wouldn't we call that cheating?

A popular television preacher suggested that God had blessed him with a parking space in the front row of the mall parking lot. He paused to thank God for freeing up the space on such a busy day. This was, to him, simply a sign of God's goodness and blessings. Once more I question the assumptions behind this prayer of thanks. Does God provide front row parking spaces for some, while thousands of others die each day in automobile accidents?

A man escapes unharmed from a building felled in Port-au-Prince in the 2010 earthquake. He stands before a reporter in front of the building and declares his gratitude that God saved him. Behind him stands a man looking over the rubble. His young daughter is buried and presumed dead inside. If God delivered the man before the microphone, why did God not deliver the little girl?

We might ask if God delivered the man, or if the man was just fortunate. I don't know. Is it possible that God miraculously intervened to save this man? Yes. It may be that God has some purpose we cannot perceive in saving this man.

When I was sixteen years old, I drove my old Ford Maverick forty-five miles per hour down a damp road. A truck was coming from the opposite direction. As the truck and I were passing, a car that had been tailgating the truck decided to pull across the street into a car wash.

IT IS in this sense that Christians rightly give thanks for everything; not because God is the *immediate* cause of all good, but because God is the *ultimate* cause of these blessings.

The driver pulled right in front of me; I had no time to stop. I slammed on my brakes and broadsided her car. These were the days before seat belt laws and I was not wearing my seat belt. Everything in my car was hurled forward at forty-five miles per hour, striking the windshield or wedging into and under the dash and getting thrown out the windows. My car was totaled, but I distinctly remember feeling something like hands holding me in place against the seat. I didn't bang my head against the windshield, and I was completely unharmed (as was the driver of the other car).

I believed then, and still believe, that God spared my life that day. I believed that there was something God wished me to accomplish. In the years since, however, I have always worn my seat belt. I don't know if I have already accomplished whatever God intends for me; I assume that next time I might not feel those hands holding me in place! Having officiated at a number of funerals for people who died in car crashes, I know that most people in collisions like the one I was in do not survive.

Back to the man from Haiti. He may have been saved by God for some purpose yet to be fulfilled. But most people who are in a building during an earthquake, or who are in a collision going forty-five miles per hour without a seat belt, will not have that experience. Does that mean God predetermined that they should suffer while others are spared?

Let's look at one more illustration that invites us to consider God's ordinary ways of working in our lives and how we might give thanks for these things.

Consider the thanksgiving given at mealtime. When we sit down to eat supper, my wife and I always pause to thank God for the meal we are about to receive. What are we thanking God for in this meal? After all, farmers grew the lettuce and tomatoes and other vegetables. These foods did not miraculously appear at our table. Truckers brought this food to our market. Employees at the store stocked the produce aisle. My

> **I DO** believe God has a plan for our lives, but not one written in stone that God forces us to follow.

wife prepared the food with the help of the people at the power company. So what are we thanking *God* for? We thank God for a world that supplies such delicious things, for the blessing of taste and the joy of eating, for farmers and truckers and grocery store stockers, and for life itself—all of these are results of God's creative and sustaining work. It is in this sense that Christians rightly give thanks for everything; not because God is the *immediate* cause of all good, but because God is the *ultimate* cause of these blessings.

DOES GOD HAVE A PLAN?

There are so many more things that can and should be said about God's providence—how God works in our world. As I was writing this chapter my wife said, "That topic is an entire book, not just one chapter," and she was right. I do not hope or presume in this chapter to provide all of the answers to perhaps the greatest theological question of all time. The truth is, I don't have it all sorted out myself. But I want to end with a word about what I believe is God's plan, and then one final example of God's relationship to suffering and when I've seen Christians get it right.

I do believe God has a plan for our lives, but not one written in stone that God forces us to follow. Much of

God's plan is fairly simple to understand. We read the Scriptures, particularly the teachings of Jesus, and we seek to follow them. In every situation, in every encounter, in every relationship, and in every decision, we seek to express the love of God, the love of neighbors, and what is just.

At the same time each of us has unique gifts and abilities and perhaps places of influence, and God's will is that we use these to do God's work. At times God places on our hearts a special call or a particular opportunity. We need to listen and say yes. But even when we have not heard or discerned a particular call, we know the teachings of Jesus about God's will and plan for our lives.

I find that each day God leads us, if we are paying attention and listening. I often feel prompted to make a call or to go here or there, and often when I pay attention to these prompts, I find myself having a conversation with someone who needed a pastor at just that moment. I may bump into someone who has been struggling and needs care. We speak of these things, not as mere coincidences, but as "God-incidents." The challenge and task are to pay attention and to listen to the whisper of God.

These God-incidents often seem to happen when I'm on airplanes. I've learned to pay attention. I was flying from San Antonio to Dallas a few weeks after the 2010 earthquake in Haiti. I had been in Port-au-Prince just a week earlier to meet with church leaders and to survey the damage so that our church could develop a strategy for early response. I sat in an aisle seat. There was an empty seat and then there was a woman sitting at the window. I looked over at her and saw that she was crying. I asked if she was okay, and she said she was just thinking about her mom, whose birthday she was flying to Dallas to celebrate. She said, "I was just thinking about how much I love her."

We struck up a conversation about our parents and our children. Somehow the conversation turned to Haiti, and I told her I had just been there. Then she asked the question that usually signals the end of a conversation: "What do you do for a living?" I told her I was a pastor and she said, "Oh," in a somewhat hesitant tone. I thought that might be the end of the conversa-

WHERE WAS God when the earthquake occurred? God was with the medical team from a church in Iowa, with the doctors and rescue workers, with the people in the caravan of semi trucks loaded with food and supplies.

tion. But a few minutes later she turned and said, "Can I ask you a question?"

"Of course, anything," I replied.

She asked, "How do you reconcile a loving God with the terrible devastation that happened in Port-au-Prince?" I sensed she had been thinking about this, and that she was asking this earnestly. This is what I told her:

"Let me first say that I don't believe God caused this earthquake. It was not meant to teach the Haitians or to punish them. We have a pretty good idea why earthquakes happen—it is not the Bible but science that helps us here." Several years ago I spent time studying the latest theories about earthquakes. I shared my understanding about them with her: "Earthquakes are the result of a process that actually cools the core of our planet, produces mountain ranges, and creates the earth's magnetic fields. Under the surface of the earth, magma is superheated at the core; it rises like hot air and then spreads and cools as it comes closer to the surface of the earth. As it spreads it carries the earth's plates, moving them. The magma cools, falls back toward the core, reheats and rises again, continuing the movement of the earth's plates. The plates rub against one another, eventually getting stuck. When the plates finally break free they release massive amounts of energy. This process appears to be essential for life on our planet."

She seemed very interested. I continued, "Port-au-Prince lies on one of those places where the plates were stuck. The damage was exacerbated by the fact that this is a very poor nation and buildings were not constructed to withstand this kind of earthquake. When human beings collide with the powerful forces of nature that allow life to be sustained on our planet, nature always wins. When you add poverty to the equation, the results are catastrophic."

I continued, "So, the question is really, where was God in Port-au-Prince when the earthquake occurred? God wasn't shaking the earth in order to kill innocent people. But I saw God in a medical team from a church in Iowa, treating people in the midst of the rubble. I saw God in the doctors and rescue workers, who were moved by the tragedy and immediately left the comfort of their homes in the States to be of help. I saw

> **CHRISTIANS**
>
> get it wrong when they attribute tragedy to the will, plan, and hand of God. But they get it right when they walk with those undergoing suffering, and when they selflessly serve their neigbors in need.

God in the people in the caravan of semi trucks loaded with food and supplies traveling between Santo Domingo and Port-au-Prince.

"God was the source not of the earthquake but of the comfort and hope people found as they buried their dead. On Wednesday night, while our team was in Port-au-Prince, there was another earthquake, and from the makeshift tents you could hear people cry out in fear. But then they quickly broke into the singing of hymns. God was their comfort and strength. For those who lost loved ones, God is the only hope that they will see their children or parents or friends again. I saw God in the generosity of my congregation who gave hundreds of thousands of dollars to aid the victims."

And then I concluded, "If you take God out of the equation in Haiti, you still have an earthquake with 200,000 people dead, but you have just removed the single most important source of comfort and hope."

She responded, "I'm Jewish, and that is the best answer I've ever heard. Thank you. That gives me hope."

Christians get it wrong when they attribute tragedy to the will, plan, and hand of God. They get it wrong when they blame victims as the cause of their own suffering. But they get it right when they walk with those undergoing suffering, and when they selflessly serve their neighbors in need. In this way they become the hands and feet and voice of God, caring for God's children in their moment of need.

CHAPTER 5

IN DEALING
WITH
HOMOSEXUALITY

A *note to the reader: You probably don't need me to tell you that the subject of this chapter is a controversial one, or that people of sincere and honest conviction differ in their thinking about it. As you read, I'd ask you to bear three things in mind. First, not all young adults agree on whether homosexuality is a valid form of sexual expression, as the responses to my request for feedback indicated. Second, most young adults do seem to agree that gay and lesbian persons deserve compassion and respect, and that too many Christians fail to show it to them. In trying to speak to and for these young adults, I am asking you to listen to and understand their convictions.*

The 2007 Barna study, released as the book *un-Christian*, found that 91% of young adults labeled Christianity "anti-homosexual," and this perception led many young adults to turn away from the church. This was substantiated in our interviews with and input from young adults at the Church of the Resurrection. John raised the issue, unsolicited, in our conversation:

> It applies a little bit more to my generation than it does to previous generations . . . issues on homosexuality. I myself am not, but at the same time, I fully support those who do choose it as their lifestyle, and for people in our generation, you know, homosexuality wasn't something that was spoken of in hushed tones, about people in back alleys. Some people were exposed to the "it's a crime against God" and "you'll burn in hell" aspect of it, but for many people in this day and age, my age or younger, we've seen it in the media, in our schools, in our communities, and it has become something that is accepted. You know, for a vast majority of people in my generation, people might not be homosexual, they might not even like the thought of homosexuality, but I know [that] almost all of the guys

I've talked to about it have said, yeah I don't see anything that's wrong with it. And trying to do things in the political process like ban gay marriage on a religious basis, trying to tell people that

> **YOUNG ADULTS** see this issue differently than their parents and grandparents do. For them, it's about excluding and hurting people they know and care for.

they're not eligible for the same rights of a man and woman just because it's man and man, to me that's just like looking at a biracial couple and saying you can have a legal union, but you can't have a marriage because one of you is black and one of you is white, and there was a day and age when that was considered a crime against God.

John captured well the sentiments of many young adults. I found it particularly interesting to hear these comments from a man who had just spent six years as an Army Airborne Ranger, given that the military and the church are among only a handful of organizations that will not hire self-avowed homosexuals.

A 2010 Pew Forum study noted what we have known for some time: young adults see homosexualiy very differently from those who came before them. Of those born after 1981, 63% felt that homosexuality should be accepted by society, while only 35% of those over 65 years of age believed the same. Even among "evangelicals," 39% of young adults indicated that homosexuality should be accepted. When asked in the same survey if homosexual relations are always wrong, 78% of Baby Boomers said yes (down from a high of 88% among this generation twenty years ago). Forty-three percent of young adults said homosexual relations are always wrong.

I am not suggesting that Christians should determine morality by survey. I am suggesting that young adults see this issue differently than their parents and grandparents do. For young people, this issue is about excluding and hurting people they know and care about. They are also much more likely to see homosexuality, not as a willful decision to act in sinful, immoral, or perverted ways, but as a natural way that a small percentage of the population is either biologically or psychologically "wired." They do not consider it offensive, immoral, or sinful when two people of the same sex love each other deeply.

Mainline churches are terribly divided over this issue. I predict that in ten to fifteen years evangelical churches will also be divided over this issue. And in twenty to twenty-five years, churches that continue to speak about homosexuality in the ways that many churches do today will have lost the larger part of a generation. The trends toward greater acceptance are not going to reverse, and this will lead many people who are currently conservative on this issue to see it differently. I believe those segments of mainline churches that are currently leaving their denominations over this issue will find themselves in an interesting, isolated position twenty years from now.

It is important to recognize how serious of an issue this is for both sides in the divide. For "traditionalists"—Christians who support the traditional views that sexual intimacy and marriage are morally appropriate only when between a man and a woman—the issue is not about just homosexuality but about the authority and role of Scripture in the life of Christians. Some Christians who are conservative on this issue are great advocates for social justice in other areas of life. Many are compassionate and welcome homosexuals into their churches. Where they struggle is with the idea of setting aside the Bible's handful of clear prohibitions against homosexual

> **IT IS**
>
> difficult for many to see how one can set aside these Scriptures and still maintain that the Bible has authority to speak in other areas of our lives.

IN AN attempt to maintain a code of moral holiness in the church, Christians sometimes speak and act in ways that do not reflect the most important component of holiness: love.

sexual intimacy and those additional passages pointing toward marriage as the union between a man and a woman.

It is difficult for these persons to see how one can set aside these scriptures and still maintain that the Bible has authority to speak in other areas of our lives. Why, they might ask, should we take seriously the scriptures on helping the poor, or tithing, or loving our enemies when we have set aside scriptures indicating that God's will is for marriage to be between a man and a woman? A great battle rages within the most compassionate of these persons between the desire to show compassion and fairness toward homosexuals and their belief that the Bible is "useful for teaching, for reproof, for correction, and for training in righteousness" (2 Timothy 3:16).

I recently had an exchange on Facebook with a man who spoke of "homophobes" and "co-dependent" preachers who were unwilling to speak the "truth." He was referring to traditionalists, but I think he did not understand the issue from the perspective of those he opposed. The use of terms like "homophobe" is not helpful in persuading others either—it inspires only defensiveness and anger.

It is true, however, that the church includes people who are insensitive, and whose agenda on this issue is far less about pleasing God than it is about power and control. In an attempt to maintain a code of moral holiness in the church, they sometimes speak and act in ways that do not reflect the most important component of holiness: love. I received this note as I was preaching the series of sermons that became this book:

> This sounds like another "trendy" teaching to water down Christianity. Sure Christians can get it wrong. But calling homosexuality a sin and telling homos they are going to hell without repentance and faith is not wrong . . . it's LOVE.

That note sure sounds loving, doesn't it?

THE BIBLE SAYS IT; I BELIEVE IT; THAT SETTLES IT?

As I have said above, when it comes to the debate over homosexuality within the Christian faith, the underlying issue is not homosexuality but the nature of Scripture and its authority for our lives. Some people cannot see how we can set aside the handful of scriptures that teach that same-sex intimacy is wrong without setting aside the whole of Scripture. It's unsettling to say that a particular moral teaching in the Scripture is no longer applicable to us. On what basis might we set aside these verses yet still maintain that the Bible is authoritative when it calls us to care for the poor, to love our enemies, and to do justice?

First, let's consider the nature of the Bible as holy Scripture, and then we will focus on a particular principle that guided Jesus' life—the principle that puts people before rules.

When I first became a Christian, my view of the Bible was fairly simplistic: Scripture is the Word of God. All Scripture was on an equal plane, and every word was chosen by God. The Bible was inerrant and infallible (without mistake and completely flawless). I was taught the slogan "The Bible says it; I believe it; that settles it."

Having read the Bible now virtually every day for more than thirty years, preaching it every weekend for twenty years, and studying it in small groups and in pursuing my own study, I am aware that the Bible is more complicated than simplistic slogans. We don't simply follow each word and apply it literally in our lives. Allow me to illustrate.

Most Christians eat pork, crab, shrimp, and, if they can afford it, lobster—all of which were forbidden by God in the Bible (see Leviticus 11:2-12). Most Christians take our Sabbath rest and day of worship on the first day of the week—Sunday—rather than on Saturday when God commanded the Israelites to observe the Sabbath (Genesis 2:2-3), and we think nothing of mowing the yard or cleaning the house on our day off. Though Paul commands that "women should be silent in the churches" (1 Corinthians 14:34), many denominations, even fundamentalist churches, now allow women, at least the pastor's wife, to speak in worship. When Jesus tells us to cut off our hands if they cause us to sin (see Matthew 5:30; Mark 9:43), we don't take him literally—we *interpret* his words. Jesus tells us not to store up treasures on earth (see Matthew 6:19-21), yet most of us have retirement

> **WHEN THE**
>
> Bible paints more than one picture of what God wants, the question is this: Did God change, or did human understanding of God change?

accounts. Is this not a violation of the actual words of Jesus?

Peter says to women, "Do not adorn yourselves outwardly by braiding your hair, and by wearing gold ornaments or fine clothing" (1 Peter 3:3); and Paul says the same in 1 Timothy 2:9: "Women should dress themselves modestly and decently in suitable clothing, not with their hair braided, or with gold, pearls, or expensive clothes." Despite these clear instructions from the Bible, many Christians do not take these teachings literally.

Beyond these teachings, passages in the Bible attribute to God actions and attitudes that seem wholly out of character with the way Jesus portrays God. The Bible commands the community to stone to death sons who are disrespectful to their parents (see Deuteronomy 21:18-21). Those who work on the Sabbath are also to be put to death (Exodus 31:12-15). If a priest's daughter becomes a prostitute, he is to burn her to death (Leviticus 21:9). How do we reconcile that with Jesus, who was a friend to prostitutes? And when God, in 1 Samuel 15:3, asks Saul to lead the armies of Israel against the Amalekites saying, "Now go and attack Amalek, and utterly destroy all that they have; do not spare them, but kill both man and woman, child and infant, ox and sheep, camel and donkey," is this really right? Did God really command that Saul destroy the Amalekites because 375 years earlier their ancestors had treated the Israelites with disrespect? Contrast this view of God with that portrayed in Luke 23:34, when Jesus (God the Son) is hanging on the cross and looks upon the Romans and the Pharisees

IS GOD

vindictive, destroying a people 375 years after an offense, or is God one who shows mercy even to the people who torture, humiliate, and hang him on a cross?

who crucified him and prays, "Father, forgive them; for they do not know what they are doing"? Is God vindictive, destroying a people 375 years after an offense, or is God one who shows mercy even to the people who torture, humiliate, and hang him on a cross?

Here's the question I ask concerning the very different pictures of God painted in 1 Samuel 15 and Luke 23: Did God change, or did human understanding of God change?

Biblical scholars speak of "progressive revelation." This is the idea that the promptings of God's Spirit were understood in the light of the concepts, ideas, and presuppositions of the times in which the biblical authors lived. This is important—Christians speak of the Bible as the "Word of God" but it was not dictated by God. Rather, it was written by people who were

I LOVE

the Bible. I carry it with me everywhere I go. I read it every day. I seek to live according to it. But I also recognize that the word of God is found in the midst of the words of humans, and these words may not adequately capture the timeless Word of God.

reflecting upon God, God's will, and God's promptings in their hearts. The authors were speaking to the people of their times, addressing current issues, needs, and challenges. Unlike any words about God in the Scripture, Jesus is the pure and complete Word of God. Thus we read all Scripture in the light of what Jesus said and did.

I love the Bible. I carry it with me everywhere I go. I read it every day. I seek to live according to it. But I also recognize that the word of God is found in the midst of the words of humans, and these words may not adequately capture the timeless Word of God. The Bible captures God's word as it was given in specific historical circumstances, understood, and recorded by authors who were shaped by and addressing their own cultures. Christians must seek to understand the Bible's teachings in the light of Jesus' own life and teachings. This is particularly true when the words of the Bible are used to exclude particular groups of people.

Let's consider one of the most important examples of a Christian leader coming to understand that a particular teaching of Scripture is not God's timeless word, and that it is time to set this teaching aside as no longer applicable.

Peter is a follower of Jesus and a Jew. His Bible is the writings of the Old Testament. In the passage we're about to read, Peter is still striving to live according to its 613 laws because "the Bible says it; I believe it; that settles it." In the tenth chapter of the book of Acts, Peter is in the town of Joppa on the southern edge of what is now Tel Aviv. He is hungry, and while his meal is being prepared, he is in prayer. As he prays, he enters into something like a trance and sees a vision. A large sheet is let down in front of him by its four corners, and inside it are all kinds of animals, reptiles, and birds that God clearly commands are not to be eaten (see Leviticus 11). God's commands prohibit even touching such animals. To touch them is to become defiled. Jews of that time did not eat pork, crab, lobster, shrimp, and a host of other things that God said were unclean. But look at Acts 10:11-15:

> [Peter] saw the heaven opened and something like a
> large sheet coming down, being lowered to the ground

by its four corners. In it were all kinds of four-footed creatures and reptiles and birds of the air. Then he heard a voice saying, "Get up, Peter; kill and eat." But Peter said, "By no means, Lord; for I have never eaten anything that is profane or unclean." The voice said to him again, a second time, "What God has made clean, you must not call profane."

In Peter's vision, he hears God telling him to do something expressly forbidden by Scripture. Peter is told to set aside a clear teaching of Scripture, and he is given permission to eat what had formerly been unclean. God says to Peter, "Do not call anything unclean that I have made clean." This passage is the beginning of something huge that God is doing.

While Peter tries to make sense of his vision, he hears a knock at the door. Three Gentiles (non-Jews) have arrived, sent by a Roman commander named Cornelius to fetch Peter. Peter goes with them to Cornelius's home. A good Jew would not have entered this home because Gentiles were considered unclean. But Peter had an epiphany. He suddenly understands: The rules are changing! Listen to how he explains his epiphany to the people in Cornelius's home, all of them Gentiles: "You yourselves know that it is unlawful for a Jew to associate with or to visit a Gentile; but God has shown me that I should not call anyone profane or unclean" (Acts 10:28).

Peter's world is changing, and he must move beyond the mind-set that says, "The Bible says it; I believe it; that settles it." Instead he says, *"The Bible says it, but I think God is up to something new, so I will listen to and follow God."*

None of this sets aside the Bible's teaching on homosexuality, but it does give us permission to ask questions: "When Leviticus 18:22 and 20:13 teach that same-sex intimacy is an abomination and, in 20:13, that those who participate in it should be put to death, does this capture the heart, character, and eternal will of God, or do these verses capture the values and reflections of a people who lived 3,200 years ago and who had little understanding of homosexuality?" Does God really want us to put homosexuals to death? When Paul writes in Romans 1:26-27 about women and men committing shameless acts with one another by giving up the "natural" form of sexual intimacy for the unnatural, was

DO WE

set aside every scripture we don't like? No, but neither do we simply quote a verse or two and consider the matter settled. Instead, we devote serious study to serious questions.

that God speaking and declaring homosexuality to be shameless and unnatural, or was it Paul describing first-century Jewish understandings of what was natural and unnatural?

Now you might rightly ask, "If we start setting aside certain scriptures, where do we stop?" That's a great question, and an important one. Do we set aside every scripture we don't like and find a rationalization for setting it aside? No, but we do engage in serious study and reflection when we are faced with serious issues, and we don't simply quote a verse or two and consider the matter settled.

John Wesley, the founder of Methodism, is said to have understood that Scripture is the primary basis for our faith and practice. It contains all that is necessary for our salvation. But he also believed that rightly interpreting and applying Scripture in life requires the benefit of the church's theological, ethical, and biblical reflections of the last 2,000 years—including the work of scholars, commentators, ethicists, and theologians. Similarly, he emphasized the role of our rational minds and scientific knowledge in our reading of Scripture. Finally, John Wesley called us to bring our life experience and the witness of the Spirit to bear upon our study, interpretation, and application of Scripture in our lives.

You may think this is all so much rationalization—I do not. I see it as the essential work of rightly handling the Scriptures. This is the process that allowed us to conclude that though slavery is allowed in the Bible, it is inconsistent with the broader message of Scripture concerning the dignity of humankind and of justice. This process allows us to conclude that though the Bible speaks of women "keeping silent in the church," the dominant biblical themes speak to the shared dignity of men and women. Both were created in the image of God, and partnership rather than male dominance is more aligned with justice.

All of this leads me to be open to the possibility that God's perspective on homosexuality may be different from what we read in Leviticus and in Paul's letter to the church at Rome. It may be that heterosexuality is God's ideal and intention for humanity; our

EVEN WHEN we are divided over the issue of homosexuality, we can agree that we wish to be the kind of church in which men and women who are gay and lesbian find the warmth and welcome and love of Jesus Christ.

bodies bear witness to this as does the Bible's teaching about God creating us male and female. But I have come to believe that God's compassion and understanding toward persons who don't fit these norms—whose fundamental wiring seems to be oriented toward same-sex attraction— are undoubtedly greater than the Scriptures indicate.

GOD'S LOVE OF PEOPLE

This understanding of the nature of Scripture opened the door for me to see this issue differently than I once had, but when I began to know and care about people who are homosexual, my heart truly changed. I pastor a congregation of 17,000 people. Assuming that persons with same-sex attractions make up 5 percent of the population, there are likely 850 people in the congregation I serve who are homosexual. Add to this the people who have family members who are gay or lesbian, and the number increases significantly. One Sunday I asked the members of our congregation to raise a hand if they had a family member, close friend, or someone they cared about who was homosexual. Nearly everyone raised their hands.

I think of Mary, whose pastor I have been since she was two years old. She's a sweet, kind, and humble young woman who grew up in our children's program, participated in our youth program, and is now attending college. She told me recently that she is homosexual. I was moved to tears as I read some of the things other Christians have said to her. I think of Aaron, who grew up in our youth group and served in leadership in our church, and who was quite serious about wanting to follow Jesus Christ. I think of Kristin, whom I watched grow up. She is now a schoolteacher and in a covenant relationship with her partner.

Many of my questions about homosexuality are yet to be answered. There are dimensions of the discussion that don't fit neatly into the arguments of the Right or the Left. But this one thing I am certain of—I don't want to lead a church that turns away young adults like Mary, Aaron, or Kristin.

There are many things about Jesus that I love. One of them is that he consistently put people before rules. He had a heart for people whom others deemed sinful. He went out of his way to touch those who were unclean, and in him they found hope and love. The Pharisees were incensed that Jesus met and ate with "sinners and tax collectors." Even the disciples were

> **ONE OF** the things I love about Jesus is that he consistently put people before rules.

a bit surprised by some of the people Jesus associated with. For Jesus, however, people came before rules.

One of my favorite stories from Jesus' ministry is found in John 4:5-39. Jesus waits at a well in Samaria and talks with a woman. You may want to read this story. It speaks volumes about Jesus' character and heart toward people whom others would have shunned. The woman has been married and divorced five times, and at this point, she's living with a man who is not her husband. This was quite scandalous in the first century. Jesus speaks to her and offers her "living water" (v. 10) so that she will "never be thirsty" (v. 14). He doesn't lecture her on the evils of divorce or cohabitation. He doesn't even say, "leave the man you are living with." He offers her grace. In response, the woman becomes the first missionary and evangelist to the Samaritans, and we read in verse 39: "Many Samaritans from that city believed in him because of the woman's testimony."

This discussion and this story lead me to an e-mail I received a couple of years ago that describes what I think it looks like when Christians get it right regarding homosexuality:

> I am a lesbian who has a partner and three children. I have never been to your church. But this e-mail is not about being gay or about the church's stance on being gay. It is about one of your members whose name is Carol. Carol lives next door to me. She was one of the

first neighbors to come and say "hello." She was warm and inviting and one day she invited us to church. . . . I told her I was gay, and she didn't raise an eyebrow or frown. I told her my father was a Southern Baptist preacher, and I hold very strong beliefs. When a church shuns me it hurts more than words can express. She invited me again to church. I checked out your church's Web site and was impressed that the church was talking about this issue and not just praying it would go away.

I have never valued a church by the number of people in the pews or the amount of money in the offering. What I am moved by is a woman so touched by your church that she came into my heart. She lives a life that so many could learn from. She opens up her home to people in need. She checks on those who aren't feeling well. And she shared Christ with a woman she knew was gay because it was in her heart to do it. I have been truly blessed by this woman, and I am hoping to visit your church in the future.

Not all Christians see the issue of homosexuality in the same way. The church is divided on this issue. But even in a divided church, we can agree that we wish to be the kind of church in which men and women who are gay and lesbian find the warmth and welcome and love of Jesus Christ. I think Christians get it wrong when they speak in ways that bring harm and alienation to God's gay children; I think we get it right when, even in our uncertainty, we express the love and welcome of the one who offered living water to the woman at the well.

CHAPTER 6

WHEN CHRISTIANS GET IT RIGHT

Christians have always struggled to "get it right." Most of the New Testament was written to Christians who were "getting it wrong." They struggled with self-righteousness, hypocrisy, judgmentalism, spiritual pride, moral compromise, and a host of other issues. The New Testament letters were often aimed at

> **IF YOU**
>
> boiled down the gospel to
> one word, it would be *love*.

correcting these things.

Underlying all of the other counsel the apostles gave for how Christians can get it right is one common refrain: To get it right is to love. Peter says it this way, "Love covers a multitude of sins" (1 Peter 4:8). James writes, "You do well if you really fulfill the royal law according to the scripture, 'You shall love your neighbor as yourself'" (James 2:8). John is even bolder in his first epistle, "Whoever does not love does not know God, for God is love" (1 John 4:8).

Among the most dysfunctional churches in the New Testament, where Christians were getting it wrong, was the church at Corinth in Greece. Their church was fractured and filled with Christians who acted in ways that scarcely resembled the Christ they claimed to follow. To these Christians, Paul writes very directly:

> If I speak in the tongues of mortals and of angels, but do not have love, I am a noisy gong or a clanging cymbal. And if I have prophetic powers, and understand all mysteries and all knowledge, and if I have all faith, so as to remove mountains, but do not have love, I am nothing. (1 Corinthians 13:1-2)

Paul goes on to describe this love that Christians are to live out:

> Love is patient; love is kind; love is not envious or boastful or arrogant or rude. It does not insist on its own way; it is not irritable or resentful; it does not rejoice in wrongdoing, but rejoices in the truth. It bears all things, believes all things, hopes all things, endures all things.
>
> Love never ends. . . . And now faith, hope, and love abide, these three; and the greatest of these is love. (1 Corinthians 13:4-8a, 13)

Why does Paul place such strong emphasis on love? Because if you boiled down the gospel to one word, it would be *love*. Jesus commands his disciples to love God with their entire being and to love their neighbors as they love themselves (see Luke 10:27). This is what biblical scholar Scott McKnight calls "the Jesus Creed." Jesus goes on to tell his disciples that the world will know that they are his disciples by their love (John 13:34-35). They are to love one another, to love their neighbor, to love those in need, and even to love their enemies.

Even as I write these words, I realize how often I fall short of them.

When Christians get it right, they practice sacrificial love. That is a powerful witness. It has the capacity to change the world.

When John came to me with his frustrations concerning the Christian faith, I did not argue with him. I listened to him and actually agreed with him. Many of the things that frustrated him also frustrated me. Others were things

> **CHRISTIANITY DOESN'T**
> invite perfect people to join up. It invites people who are prone to get it wrong and then offers them grace.

of which I had been guilty.

As I have addressed these various issues with Christians, some people get defensive. Others nod their heads. Some want to argue theology, while others say, "That's what I've always thought."

It is important to note that Christians don't have a corner on the market when it comes to getting things wrong. Muslims, Jews, Hindus, and Buddhists have gotten it wrong. Atheists and agnostics get it wrong in many of the same ways Christians get it wrong. Getting it wrong is not simply a function of theology but of our psychology, our sociology, and ultimately of our human condition. Christians call this condition *sin* though you may have another name for it. We are all afflicted with the tendency to get it wrong. The seven deadly sins are universal temptations, not unique to Christians—lust, gluttony, greed, indifference, hurting others, envy, and pride—we all struggle with these temptations.

That leads me to another point. Christianity is about forgiveness, not perfection. Jesus was unnerving to the

religious elite because he spent most of his time w
"sinners." Of course, both the priests and the prostitutes
were sinners. The difference was that the prostitutes
knew they were sinners; the priests acted as though they
were not. It seems clear in reading the Gospels that
between sexual sins and religious hypocrisy Jesus considered religious hypocrisy far more deadly.

It should be no surprise that Christians sometimes get
it wrong—Christianity doesn't invite perfect people to
join up. It invites people who are prone to get it wrong
and then offers them grace. As one person told me, "If I
never got it wrong, I would not need Christianity!"

It's important, however, for Christians to remember
that the Christian spiritual life—the life of discipleship—
does not stop at forgiveness. The aim of the Christian life is to get it right. Theologians call this process
sanctification—a word that means to be made holy. What does holi-ness look like? It looks like love. Over time, Chris-tians should be-come more loving if we are growing in our faith. The

> **OVER TIME,**
> Christians should become more loving if we are growing in our faith. The proof of spiritual growth is found in the practice of love.

111

g in the Christian faith is not found in
e Bible people have memorized or how
theology is. It is not even how well they
re obvious sins. The proof of spiritual
growth is found in the practice of love.

All Christians get it wrong some of the time, but I have
had the joy of watching many Christians working to get
it right.

Some time ago Vincent began attending our church.
He's a gifted vocalist in his thirties who sang heavy
metal and classic rock for years. Vincent is also afflicted with Tourette's syndrome. His form of
Tourette's is known as *coprolalia*, and includes the
spontaneous utterance of words that most people sup-
press—swear words. Vincent was diagnosed when he
was an adolescent. From that time on he had felt
unwelcome in church. We have a large sanctuary, but it
was easy to tell when Vincent was present, starting
with his first visit. As I was preaching he would blurt
out swear words. It was a little unnerving at first. Some
with children who did not understand what was hap-
pening moved to another part of the sanctuary. But
almost instantly some people realized that Vincent had
Tourette's. When Vincent showed up for worship, a
group of people sat near him and reassured him it was
okay. Vincent thought that perhaps it would help if

people knew his story, so one weekend we told his story and then invited him to sing. When he was finished singing about his life, the congregation rose to their feet in a standing ovation that lasted for several minutes. What they were saying to Vincent was, "We love you. We want you here. You are a gift from God!"

As they stood applauding I saw the church as it is meant to be, a community of people who welcome others with genuine love. They got it right.

Chuck, one of our members, told me a story about two other congregations who got it right. It was June 18, 1999. Chuck, his wife, Angie, and their two little boys were driving down I-24, between Jasper and South Pittsburg, Tennessee, on their way to visit Angie's

JESUS TOLD his disciples they were to be light for the world, a city upon a hill that could not be hidden. They were to let their light shine by pursuing acts of kindness, mercy, and love. In this way Christ's followers were to incarnate—to embody and make visible—the love of God for humankind.

folks. Chuck started to change lanes, noticed a car in his blind spot, and pulled the steering wheel back. As he did he lost control of the car and it spun around several times, then rolled over, crushed Angie's side of the car, and rolled over two more times before stopping. When the car finally came to a standstill, Chuck quickly looked to the backseat. The boys were fine, but crying. Then Chuck looked over at Angie. He could see she was unconscious and bleeding. He struggled to remove her seat belt. Within minutes the ambulance arrived. Angie and Chuck were taken in two separate ambulances to the hospital. Sometime later the chaplain from the hospital came to speak with Chuck. He told her that Angie had not survived the accident.

The chaplain had called the pastors of the two Baptist churches nearby—in Jasper and Pittsburg. Soon the pastor from Jasper, the pastor's wife from Pittsburg, and a group of laypeople were there at the hospital. Some had taken off from work to come and help. They went to the store to replace the bloodstained clothes Chuck was wearing and bought an overnight change of clothes for him and the boys. They brought toys and diapers and kept the kids while the pastor and others sought to comfort and care for Chuck. Chuck told me that eleven years later he is still overwhelmed by the generosity and love he felt from these Christians toward a stranger from Kansas. The folks from these two churches in Jasper and Pittsburg got it right that night.

Chris and his wife, Tammi, a remarkable young couple I know, moved from the suburbs to one of the most crime-ridden neighborhoods in Kansas City. Drive-by shootings, sexual assault, and drug houses are a nearly daily part of life in their community. But they felt called to move there to bring hope to the children and youth who live there. They started the Hope Center, which is seeking to transform the neighborhood and the children there. Today hundreds of people are finding hope through the education programs, medical clinic, and youth groups Chris and Tammi have launched. Chris and Tammi are Christians who get it right.

I have watched as people do the most giving and sacrificial things caring for one another in the church. Lori's husband, Jerry, was 1,000 miles away at M. D. Anderson Cancer Center where he was battling cancer. She was trying to care for her children, hold herself together, and give hope to her husband. She described her friends who mowed the yard, watched her children, assembled a playground in the backyard at midnight on Christmas Eve, and flew to Houston to be with her to help her and her husband through the crisis.

She told me she did not know how she could have made it without this care. That's what it looks like when Christians get it right.

CHRISTIANS ARE

not meant to repel people from God, but by their very lives to draw people to God.

There was Amy, who saw a young, pregnant teenager leaving McDonald's without a winter coat on a cold Kansas City evening. Amy ran to her car, got her own coat, and gave it to the girl, beginning a relationship with a teenage mother who needed a friend.

There was David, who saw a young man in a suit walking home from work in the rain. He stopped to give him a ride and discovered the young man walked two miles each way to work in the only suit he owned. The next morning David dropped off a bicycle and began a relationship with the young man that culminated in the young man receiving a scholarship to go to college.

Greg used the influence of his construction company to help break down racial barriers in Kansas City. Danielle and JT spent the first year of their married life in South Africa seeking to serve people in extreme poverty. Karla leads hundreds of people in visiting the forgotten people—the nursing home residents no one else ever visits at thirty area nursing homes. I think of the many people who volunteer in our Matthew's Ministry, serving more than one hundred special-needs children, youth, and adults and providing respite for their parents. They give up their weeknights and weekends to throw parties, lead groups, and to love our special-needs members. These are all Christians who get it right.

I could fill a lengthy book with stories like this. I'm not suggesting that only Christians do these things. I know others who do the same. But in my travels to Honduras and Haiti, to Zambia and South Africa, to the Gulf Coast after Hurricane Katrina and to the inner city in Kansas City, nearly all of the people I have met doing humanitarian work are Christians. Christians often get it wrong, but tens of millions of quiet Christians daily seek, without fanfare or accolades, to get it right.

Jesus told his disciples they were to be light for the world, a city upon a hill that could not be hidden. They were to let their light shine by pursuing acts of kindness, mercy, and love. In this way Christ's followers were to incarnate—to embody and make visible—the love of God for humankind. In doing this they would become the evidence of God to the world. Christians are not meant to repel people from God, but by their very lives to draw people to God.

And that leads me to one final story. I was driving to church on Martin Luther King Jr. weekend, listening to an interview on NPR with the Reverend Billy Kyles. Billy was with Dr. King as he stood on the balcony of the Lorraine Motel in Memphis the morning he was killed. The interviewer asked what Rev. Kyles was preaching on that morning. He told the story of Robert Louis Stevenson who, as a boy, was sitting by his window looking intently outside. These were the days of gas streetlights and there, at the street, was the town lamplighter. He was carefully putting his ladder up against the lamppost, climbing up the ladder, and lighting the lantern. He would take it down, move down the street, and light the next one. Stevenson was asked, "What are you looking at so intently?" To which he replied, "I'm watching that man out there knock holes in the darkness."

This is what Jesus called his followers to do. It is what the church is meant to be about. By our acts of kindness and love we are called to knock holes in the darkness. I think young adults need to see Christians get it right. They need to see Christians knocking holes in the darkness. When they do, there's little doubt that they will be interested once again in the gospel that inspires such actions.

If you've been turned off by Christians you've known, I'd invite you, as I did John, to get to know the real Jesus by reading one of the earliest accounts of his life and teachings. Read the Gospel According to Luke. It was as I read that Gospel as a teenager that I decided to follow this remarkable man. There are churches out there who seek to get it right. They are not perfect, but you would find in them a community of people who will welcome you, who will help you to know more about Jesus, and who will invite you to join them in knocking holes in the darkness.

POSTSCRIPT

....

You may be wondering what happened with John. After our initial conversation, I asked John if he would come back and allow me to interview him before a camera so that I could share his perspectives both with my own congregation and with a broader audience of church leaders. Later that year he attended worship with us—it was the first time he'd been in church in years. Sometime later he asked if I would officiate at his wedding. I was honored that he asked, and I had the joy of sitting down with John and Nancy in preparation for their wedding. I enjoyed celebrating their union. In preparing this book, I asked John to read it and give me his feedback.

Has John become a Christian? No, not yet. I sense an openness I did not see the first time we met. And though we don't get the chance to talk often, I believe he values our relationship as do I. My hope and prayer is that one day he will become a follower of Jesus Christ.

This book is dedicated to him.

Also by Adam Hamilton

"Adam Hamilton is a thoughtful man whose writings will stretch your mind and heart."

—**BILL HYBELS**, Senior Pastor, Willow Creek Community Church and Chairman of the Board, Willow Creek Association

"When you list the best-known names in American Christianity—Billy Graham, Bill Hybels, Rick Warren, Max Lucado, Jim Wallis, and others—you probably don't yet think of Adam Hamilton. But you should, and I believe you will in the future. He combines a deep theological mind with an accessible, effective communicative style, growing from the platform of a truly innovative and exemplary church. I pay attention to everything he writes, and I hope his influence will expand dramatically with this new book."

—**BRIAN MCLAREN**,
Author/Activist, brianmclaren.net

"We desperately need voices that can teach us to combine passionate conviction with charitable civility and honest self-examination. Adam Hamilton is one of those thoughtful voices, and *Seeing Gray* will help that conversation."

—**JOHN ORTBERG**, Author of *When the Game Is Over It All Goes Back In the Box*

Also by Adam Hamilton

Walk with Jesus on his final day.

Sit beside him at the Last Supper.

Pray with him in Gethsemane.

Follow him to the cross.

Desert him. Deny him.

Experience the Resurrection.

No single event in human history has received more attention than the suffering and crucifixion of Jesus of Nazareth. In this heartbreaking, inspiring book, Adam Hamilton guides us, step by step, through the last 24 hours of Jesus' life.

"Adam Hamilton combines biblical story, historical detail, theological analysis, spiritual insight, and pastoral warmth to retell the narrative of Jesus' last and greatest hours."

—LEITH ANDERSON

author of *The Jesus Revolution*

 Abingdon Press